He aha te mea nui o te ao?
He tangata, he tangata, he tangata.

What is the most important thing in the world?
It is the people, it is the people, it is the people.

~Māori proverb

HOW TO MOVE TO NEW ZEALAND

in 31 Easy Steps

Sara Dawn Johnson

Force Four Publications

Copyright © 2016 Sara Dawn Johnson

Force Four Publications
411 Walnut St. #8630
Green Cove Springs, FL 32043
www.forcefourpubs.com

ISBN: 978-0-9971358-3-1 (paperback)
ISBN: 978-0-9971358-2-4 (eBook)

Library of Congress Control Number: 2016916706

Fonts used in this book:
Oil Change by Jay Hilgert @ Albatross
Gemelli by Jason Pagura (1001fonts.com)
Rudiment by Kevin Richey (1001fonts.com)
Palatino by Hermann Zapf

Cover art by: Ravindu Tharanga Perera

To Leah and Holly.

My reasons for everything.

Contents

Disclaimer

I am not a lawyer or immigration adviser of any kind. This book describes our family's voyage down the New Zealand immigration path. Nothing in this book shall be deemed advice or guarantee for anyone else's immigration path. Neither I nor the publisher assume any responsibility or liability for actions taken by readers of this book.

Your particular circumstances—not limited to age, nationality, and professional credentials—may be different than ours. While the immigration path I describe is similar to that of many others, every immigrant has their own variation. If you require specific advice, please consult with an immigration lawyer or licensed immigration adviser.

In addition, immigration laws and regulations change continually; what I describe in this book is current as of September 2016. I do not assume any responsibility for errors, omissions, or interpretations of the information included. I strive to keep this book updated and welcome any input from readers who encounter new information in the course of moving to New Zealand. Please contact me at sara@saradawnjohnson.com with updates and let me know if it is okay to use your name in a revised edition.

From our family to yours: we wish you the best of luck in your move to New Zealand, the greatest little country in the world.

Sara Dawn Johnson
Wellington, New Zealand
September, 2016

Introduction

January 2009, the United States: A fire glows in our family room wood stove. I'm sure it was raining outside, just on the edge of freezing as it does all through the winter months in the Pacific Northwest. My husband, Michael, and I have just finished tucking our 3-year-old daughter, Leah, into her bed upstairs. We let ourselves sink into the overstuffed green corduroy couch near the fire. Our infant daughter, Holly, lay sleeping in my arms. We press play on the DVD remote.

We were finally getting around to watching something we'd received a few weeks earlier, Michael Palin's *Around the World in 80 Days*, a BBC travel series from the 1980s Netflix recommended for us. Two discs in and our lives were changed forever. Palin's goal was to make it around the world in 80 days or less using only land or sea travel, just as in Jules Verne's classic novel of the same name. Palin's adventures were fascinating and funny and on that comfortable and cosy green couch we realised we wanted the same.

By the last episode, when Palin makes it back to London with only hours to spare, we'd decided to leave our little home in the woods and take our family out into the world. We craved adventure, new foods, new languages, and new friends. We would travel how Palin did in much of his around-the-world adventure: by sea.

While we'd been living on land for the past couple of years, Michael and I had spent the previous ten years together afloat. We'd lived aboard several different sailing boats, all the while working to save money, fixing up our boat, and sailing. In April 2000 we got hitched and then spent the following summer meandering up the inside passage to Alaska. Two years later we turned left out of Washington's Puget Sound and made our way down the west coast of the United States to Mexico, where we spent the winter before returning to Seattle for work.

When Leah was born in 2006, we brought her home to the boat as a newborn. By the time she was nine months old, winter was on the way and I needed a break from the cold and damp dock life and so we moved ashore. We always dreamt of finding our way to the sea again and watching Palin make his way around the world sparked something in us.

It was time to stop dreaming and start planning.

Five years earlier, during the winter season we spent in Mexico, we made fast friends with several boat crews also in their 20s. For months we travelled together. Diving, road trips, potlucks, happy hours...it was an idyllic time. At the end of the season, we had our 35-foot boat trucked up to Seattle while several boat crews either stayed another year in Mexico or sailed across the South Pacific and on to New Zealand. We seriously considered doing the same, but decided our funds were too low and our boat too old to make the trip.

Ever since, despite having built a beautiful family and home, a big chunk of our souls regretted not sailing to New Zealand. We often wondered what our lives would look like had we done so. Would we have found the South Pacific to be as beautiful as we'd heard? Would we have enjoyed living in a foreign land—one that is exotic and fresh and friendly?

And then that winter, inspired by watching travel tales by the fire, tantalized by the thought of giving the gift of travel to our daughters, we thought: why not now?

That was all it took for our dream to change to a plan. We would sell our house and quit our jobs, buy another boat, and sail it across the South Pacific and on to New Zealand where we'd make a new home. And in the end, we did just that.

Of course, the path to New Zealand wasn't quite so straightforward and easy to navigate. There were hurdles along the way. Perhaps the most significant of them came in the form of doubt, expressed by others, that we'd be successful building a new life somewhere else.

"There are no jobs in New Zealand."

"It's impossible to get a visa there."

"You guys are too old."

"Your health is not good enough."

Surprisingly, we learned that the skeptics only firmed our resolve. I guess you could say there wasn't any stopping us until it was done.

Following lots of paperwork, some fees, a lot of waiting and hand-wringing and stress, in 2013, the beautiful, friendly, and peaceful little country of New Zealand granted us residence. This gave us the rights to live, work, vote, enjoy the protection of affordable socialised healthcare, and attend public school—all for as long as we like.

Since then I've received countless emails from friends and blog readers asking how we did it. I wrote a blog post[1] in 2013 describing the steps we took to gain residence. That post remains my most-read article in 17 years of travel blogging. I continue to get email weekly from people all over the world who want additional details on the immigration process. I pointed several readers to helpful resources and sent words of encouragement before finally deciding to capture everything I know about moving to New Zealand, in great detail, in this book. I share my tips for where to start on the visa process, how to enrol kids in school, and how to get the most out of living in this small, fascinating country.

New Zealand is a nation of immigrants and continues to warmly welcome people from around the world. In cities like Auckland and Wellington,

---

[1] http://www.svwondertime.com/2013/07/03/how-to-move-to-new-zealand-in-31-easy-steps/

English and Māori are widely spoken, but I'm likely to hear also Hindi, Bengali, Chinese, Japanese, Tagalog, Tongan, French, Spanish, and German. Our eldest daughter attended a central Auckland primary school and we now have friends from South Africa, Pakistan, India, Philippines, Ireland, and China.

Are you ready to join the mix? You can do it, in 31 easy steps—don't let anyone tell you otherwise.

Step 1:
Things to Consider
Before You Go

New Zealand lives up to all the country's ac-
claims, but there are challenges to living in a
small island nation at the bottom of the world. You
should be aware of these challenges and consider
them realistically before you pack up and head
down to join us here.

New Zealand is very, very far away

We are nearly 7,000 miles from our former home
on the west coast of the United States, and over
11,000 miles from London. It takes 12 hours to
fly from Auckland to Los Angeles—never mind
any necessary connecting flights on either end.
It's 28 hours to London. And international flights
from New Zealand aren't cheap (an economy
round-trip ticket from Auckland to LA or London costs roughly NZ$2,000 per adult). Should
you decide to ship household goods to New Zealand, sea freight is cost-effective, but it can take
months for your goods to arrive.

You'll have to lock up your pet

New Zealand is rabies-free and wants to keep it
that way. Accordingly, they enforce a strict,

complicated, and costly pet importing process[2]. If you have a cat or dog (sorry, no birds, reptiles, or ferrets allowed) that you simply can't bear to leave behind, be prepared for micro-chipping, vaccinations, blood tests, parasite treatments, an import permit, and at least a 10-day quarantine for your pet. Total fees, including airfare for one cat or dog, can easily add up to NZ$4,000-6,000.

Stuff is expensive

All the rumours you've heard are true: goods and services in New Zealand are expensive. We pay far more for food than we ever did in the United States (even for locally grown and produced food, which nobody can explain). Of course, much of what Kiwis consume is imported, so retail prices reflect the simple costs of getting stuff here from elsewhere, as well as import duty. GST (goods and services tax) of 15% is also added to nearly every purchase and service. We can order things directly from overseas retailers (Amazon.com will ship many items to New Zealand) but shipping costs can be quite high for heavier and larger items. Even a small, cheap-to-ship, expensive electronic item (such as an iPad) that we can buy online at a lower cost from overseas, will get dinged on import duty and GST charges when it passes through New Zealand Customs. But don't despair. If the high cost of

---

[2] http://mpi.govt.nz/importing/live-animals/pets/

things gets you down, you can always pour
yourself a glass of New Zealand wine to ease the
pain—it's one of the few values, inexpensive and
delicious.

Housing is in crisis

New Zealanders are facing major housing problems[3] in terms of affordability, availability, and
quality. Uncontrolled speculation, low interest
rates, and liberal mortgage lending practices
have driven prices sky-high in the larger cities,
particularly Auckland. Rents are rising as well,
but not as quickly as housing prices, thankfully.
(We are renting a waterfront house near Wellington for a fraction of the amount of a mortgage payment on the property.) But renters in
New Zealand are pretty much relegated the status of squatters—only there to keep owners' investment properties aired out. Landlords are
given far more rights than tenants; almost no
cause or explanation is required from a landlord
who wants to raise the rent or evict tenants, for
example. Many dwellings are of poor quality.
It's common to see single-pane windows, no
heating systems, and little or no insulation. Additionally, electricity prices countrywide rise
sharply during the cold months. The good news
is that new laws are coming into effect and will
require landlords to insulate rental properties

[3]http://www.labour.org.nz/housing_crisis_affecting_more_than_98_
per_cent_of_nz

and provide efficient heating in main living areas. (See Step 15 for more on selecting housing.)

Wages and salaries are low

Stagnant wages are a worldwide phenomenon, but New Zealanders are facing a particular struggle with wages and salaries not keeping pace with rising expenses. Lack of union bargaining power, reduced government regulations, a low minimum wage, and international outsourcing are contributing causes[4]. What this means is that in New Zealand, you might not make as much money as you would in Seattle or San Francisco or Sydney, Australia, but you'll be rewarded with an excellent quality of life instead.

After presenting a list like that, I have to remind you that all the good is *really* good. The landscape is as stunning as all the photos and movies show. There are breathtaking beaches, mountains, rivers, forests, waterfalls, caves, glaciers, lakes, birds, and giant insects. Even better, the people of New Zealand outshine the natural beauty. Strangers smile and say hello as they pass. People help people when needed, without question. Neighbours chat over fences or in the grocery store or at the corner coffee shop.

---

[4] http://www.stuff.co.nz/dominion-post/comment/5824465/New-Zealanders-get-low-wages

Here are some aspects of New Zealand that have pleasantly surprised us:

Pohutukawas

These native trees are found throughout the country, from city parks to beaches. Most of the year, they are green and bushy. But in early December, a few weeks before Christmas and…KAPOW! They burst forth with bright red, fluffy flowers. These New Zealand "Christmas trees" are the prettiest we've ever seen.

Christmas at the beach

Despite retailers' continued efforts, Christmas here is less about the stuff and more about spending time with family, usually at the beach and followed with a sausage sizzling on the grill. The Christmases of my childhood were always huge affairs with decorations everywhere, elaborate meals, parties, piles of gifts; my mother no doubt took years off her life preparing for it all. Not me. In stark contrast to the American Christmas, I love the simplicity of a New Zealand Christmas: a few basic decorations, a couple of gifts for our daughters from Santa, and a day spent with friends and family, under the sun and with sandy toes. It helps that summer break from school starts a few days before Christmas, a time of year so good that it even has the best name ever: Silly Season.

Bare feet

Even in the city and at primary school, shoes are completely optional!

Southernmost Polynesia

The islands of Aotearoa (the original Māori name for New Zealand) are the southernmost Polynesian islands (the Hawaiian islands are northernmost). Māori culture is very similar to Marquesan culture (it is believed the Māori came from eastern Polynesia originally). Auckland is the largest Polynesian city and not only does a large Māori population call it home, but so do Tahitians, Cook Islanders, Tongans, Samoans, Niueans, and Fijians. The food, music, art, tattoos and colour of Polynesia are all around.

Legends

Aotearoa is a land of myth and legend: the taniwhas, Tāne Mahuta, Maui, Kupe, the first wakas to sail to New Zealand from Hawaiki. Māori stories live rich in this land and are interwoven into everyday life. When we walk through a great forest, or gaze out at the Tasman sea from a cliff top, the spirit of the land is omnipresent and it's easy to feel why this is the land of story.

Language

On a planet where languages are disappearing at an alarming rate, it's so refreshing to see te reo Māori, the original language of New Zealand, being studied and celebrated and respected. Our daughters learn Māori words and songs at school, universities offer tuition-free classes in Māori, and there is an entire TV station that broadcasts primarily in te reo Māori (maoritelevision.com). Coming from a place where people are denigrated for speaking a language other than English, it's a joy to see multilingualism celebrated and promoted.

Schools

New Zealand schools are not bogged down in standards and testing and constant evaluations as are United States and U.K. schools. While general curriculum guidelines exist, schools are free to experiment, to adjust their teaching methods to suit students' specific needs, and to incorporate new ideas at a rapid pace. Outside time and sport are highly valued. In fact, nearly all students are taught to swim and many primary schools have their own pools. Schools welcome help and input from parents. There are no metal detectors or intruder drills. The result is that both our daughters love school and think learning is great fun. What more could we want? Well, we also take comfort in the fact that New Zealand universities are extremely affordable compared to colleges in the United States. For the amount of money we'd spend for a single semester at a public university in the United States, we could pay for an entire degree in New

Zealand. Furthermore, many of the programmes available at Kiwi universities are world-class.

An unarmed society

Want to know the most shocking thing we Americans learned after arriving in New Zealand? Not even the police carry handguns. Cops walk down the streets firearm-free (for serious crimes, they call in the Armed Offenders Squad). Though New Zealand is not a land of guns, it's not gun-free. A New Zealander can purchase a gun, but only after the rigorous application, education, and interview process that are required to obtain a necessary firearms licence. Guns themselves are tightly controlled and monitored. As a result, gun crime is extremely rare. Recent data show[5] that for every 100,000 New Zealanders there were 1.07 deaths by firearm (0.84 of them suicides, unfortunately). For every 100,000 Americans? Over 10.

Universal healthcare

Everyone—even legal visitors to New Zealand—is automatically covered in the case of accidental injury, thanks to the Accident Compensation Corporation or ACC (acc.co.nz). Break your leg bungee-jumping off the Kawarau bridge in Queenstown? Head to the hospital to get fixed up...for free. Most people who hold a long-term

---

[5] https://en.wikipedia.org/wiki/List_of_countries_by_firearm-related_death_rate

visa are eligible for publicly funded (non-accident-related) health services, including general practitioner (GP) care, prescriptions, hospital visits, and more. Fees are reasonable (kids under 13 are fee-free) and Kiwis don't even know what a deductible is!

Excellent work/life balance

New Zealanders are given by law four—count 'em!—FOUR weeks of paid leave per year PLUS sick leave. A typical work week is 37 hours and the culture doesn't encourage overtime. Most people take their leave over the Christmas break/school summer holidays. We've found that people take their leisure and family time, travel, hobbies, and sport much more seriously than they do their work lives.

Liberal society

If you are offended by f-bombs on the radio in the middle of the day or naked breasts on your television after the kids are in bed, well, you should probably keep your radio and TV turned off in New Zealand because no one else here seems to mind. New Zealand was the first country in the world to allow women to vote. Same-sex marriage has been legal since 2013[6]. The first time we visited the local sailors' pub to grab a pint and a bite to eat, we stepped tentatively into

---

[6] Don't miss the moving coverage of NZ Parliament breaking into a Māori love song after voting equal marriage rights into law: https://www.youtube.com/watch?v=q9pOJ8Bc_-g

the dusty dim room and asked whether our kids were welcome inside. "Sure," the barkeep said, "as long as they don't drink or smoke!" (You do have to be 18 to actually drink or smoke.)

Tasty food

Cows are grass-fed, chickens are free range. And it must be due to all the UV here that New Zealand produce is the best we've had, anywhere. Even the Chinese gooseberries[7].

---

[7] https://en.wikipedia.org/wiki/Kiwifruit

Step 2:
Get Advice

So you still want to move to New Zealand? Of course you do. But how do you get started? I'm happy to report that the second step is an easy one. Just bookmark these two websites:

- **Immigration New Zealand:** immigration.govt.nz
- **New Zealand Now:** newzealandnow.govt.nz

Both sites are maintained by the New Zealand government and offer an answer to any question you can think of regarding immigrating to New Zealand. The problem is that there is a lot of information on these websites and finding information is not easy. We spent many hours reading through the Immigration NZ website during our application process. There are tools to explore the different visa options, online applications, as well as downloadable applications and form instructions. The New Zealand Now website does a much better job explaining the different types of visas (visit/study/work/invest/refugee/family). Spend some time exploring both of them.

If you can't find what you need in the extensive knowledge base, don't hesitate to contact Immigration NZ directly (you'll find contact information at the bottom of each website). We've received timely, helpful answers to both our emailed and phoned queries.

As you'll see by exploring these immigration websites, there are many paths to gaining permanent residence. Our family's path (from visitor to work to resident) is the most common route (most immigrants we know have followed a nearly identical visa trail) and the one I focus on in this book. I'll note here that we did all the paperwork and jumped through all the hoops ourselves, and I suspect if you've bought this book, you're considering managing the process yourself as well. But that's not the only approach.

Perhaps you've read everything about immigrating to New Zealand, asked questions, received answers, and a unique wrinkle in your personal circumstances means you're still flummoxed about the process. Perhaps you're overwhelmed by the required paperwork and required evidence. Perhaps you're simply averse to the process and would prefer a bit of handholding? For all of the above, help is available in the form of a *licensed immigration adviser*. This is an expert who can help you navigate the process with your specific scenario in mind.

Specially trained licensed immigration advisers can legally provide assistance at all levels, from helping you select the correct visa to completing your application for you. If you're unsure whether you'll need an adviser, you can get started on the process on your own and engage an adviser as needed to clear a roadblock at any step along the way. Fees vary widely, depending on the level of a particular adviser's expertise to the level of complexity and urgency of a particular application.

For more information, or to hire an adviser, begin at the Immigration Advisers Authority website: iaa.govt.nz. You'll find information on the type of services they offer as well as an adviser database.

There are other sources of immigration advice and assistance as well. These include lawyers (both in New Zealand and overseas), Community Law Centres, and Citizens Advice Bureaus (cab.org.nz). Citizens Advice Bureaus in particular are amazing resources in New Zealand communities. They offer free advice, information, and guidance—on matters of immigration, consumer problems, employment and more—for anyone who needs it. Additionally, Justices of the Peace are regularly available for basic legal advice and document certifying.

In our immigration journey, we were able to sort out our visas by reading the government websites, talking to Immigration NZ directly, and asking questions of other recent immigrants. We did have a question regarding health requirements and found a friend of a friend who is an immigration adviser. He gave us the answer—and encouragement—we needed, gratis. That's the Kiwi way.

Step 3:
Get Going on the Job Search

If you plan to work in New Zealand, the time to start looking into getting a job is long before you arrive. While you may not begin your official job search until you are in the country, there are a number of things you can do to kick-start the process.

We were still in Tonga, aboard our sailboat, and not planning to arrive in New Zealand for another three months, when my husband, Michael, polished up his curriculum vitae (CV) and sent it along to friends in Auckland. They forwarded it to their information and communications technology (ICT) contacts and to recruiters with whom they'd worked. A number of the recipients responded immediately, asking Michael to get in touch again when he landed in country. Although it felt like he was jumping the gun at the time, the tactic appears to have worked. Within a week of arriving at the Bay of Islands, Michael had a job interview scheduled in Auckland and a job offer in hand a few weeks later.

Getting a job in New Zealand is a lot like anywhere else. It's all about who you know. I'd say it's even more so in New Zealand as there is only a degree or two of separation between people due to the small population. This is a tight-knit country. So if you do know someone down here, it may pay to leverage that contact.

On the other hand, it's certainly not required to know anyone. Michael landed his current ICT gig by applying for positions advertised on seek.co.nz, the most thorough job listing website in New Zealand and Australia. This is the best place to start researching the jobs that are available and where they're located. (See Step 11 for choosing which part of the country to live in.) Many New Zealand companies advertise open positions on LinkedIn.com.

My other favourite job listing sites are:

- Trade Me (all types): trademe.co.nz/jobs[8]
- New Kiwis (all types of skilled work): newkiwis.co.nz
- Kiwi Health Jobs: kiwihealthjobs.com
- NZ Education Gazette (teaching positions): www.edgazette.govt.nz

For an extensive list of job websites, browse careers.govt.nz/job-hunting/job-vacancy-and-recruitment-websites/. Check out the rest of careers.govt.nz too. It's chock-o-block full of job hunting, training, and general career advice for New Zealanders.

---

[8] You may as well bookmark trademe.co.nz right now; it's New Zealand's mashup of eBay and craigslist. You'll be using this website to find everything from a job to a flat to a car to a couch.

Finally, check out the government's Skill Shortage Lists (skillshortages.immigration.govt.nz). On these, you'll find occupations that New Zealand needs more people to fill, either temporarily or long-term. If your occupation (or one of them) is on one of the skill shortage lists, your work or residence visa application is much more likely to get approved, and more quickly.

This leads to one of the most common questions people ask me: Do I need to be in New Zealand to get a job? The answer is…it depends. If your occupation is on the skill shortage lists, you are much more likely to be successful in applying and interviewing from out of country. But even if your occupation is not in demand, and you find a job that's a perfect fit for you, apply.

According to one hiring manager I spoke to, they often interview applicants who are outside New Zealand. He says: "It's difficult to find people already here that have the ICT skills we're looking for. After we offer the person the position, they start the work visa application process. When their visa is approved, they move down and start working."

For some positions, such as seasonal or temporary work, you are likely to have a better chance at scoring a job if you interview face-to-face. As I wrote earlier, Michael began seriously applying for work after arriving in New Zealand, but having a good idea of what's available with a CV ready to go was key in making this painful process as short as possible.

In Step 10 we really got going on the job search but first we had to get here.

Step 4:
Consider Setting Up a
Business, Studying, or a
Working Holiday

*W*hat if you are just not the working-for-the-man type? Or at least—not yet? New Zealand offers visa options for people who want to come here to study, under-30s who'd like a working holiday, and for entrepreneurs to start or buy a business.

Study in New Zealand

With around 30 universities, polytechnics, and other tertiary institutions, New Zealand has a lot of options when it comes to study (see: study-innewzealand.govt.nz). The qualifications offered are internationally recognised and New Zealand universities are highly ranked in worldwide surveys[9]. Students come from all around the world to study here. As in most places, international students pay un-subsidised fees and these can be substantial. (New Zealand residents and citizens pay subsidised fees which are much lower.) The good news is many bachelor degrees take only three years to complete. There are many qualification

---

[9] http://www.topuniversities.com/subject-rankings/2016

levels, from certificates to doctoral degrees, all based on the New Zealand Qualifications Framework (NZQF)[10]. Once you complete your qualification, Immigration NZ provides a pathway[11] for international students who want to stay and work in the country and potentially gain residence.

Have a Working Holiday

If you are under 30 years old, you may be eligible for a Working Holiday Visa[12]. This visa is typically valid for 12 months and allows holders to work a temporary or seasonal job while exploring this beautiful country. It's a great way to pick up some cash while travelling and to learn whether you might want to stay long-term. We've known young people who have sailed to New Zealand, picked up a working holiday visa and easily found gigs working at restaurants, sailing on tourist ships, and working on boats. Six months later— travel kitty full—they sailed off to explore more South Pacific islands.

Be an Entrepreneur

In addition to visas based on employment or study, New Zealand offers Entrepreneur Work

---

[10] http://www.nzqa.govt.nz/studying-in-new-zealand/understand-nz-quals/

[11] https://www.newzealandnow.govt.nz/studying-in-nz/after-you-graduate

[12] https://www.immigration.govt.nz/new-zealand-visas/options/work/thinking-about-coming-to-new-zealand-to-work/working-holiday-visa

and Resident Visas[13] for those who prefer to do their own thing. If you've got the entrepreneurial spirit, investment capital, and experience, this may be your path to New Zealand residence.

According to the 2016 World Bank survey[14], New Zealand is the easiest country in the world to start a business and in which to do business. You don't have to start from scratch either; there are lots of opportunities to purchase an existing business or franchise. Adam and Cynthia Wellman purchased a property management business in Auckland in 2011. They were granted permanent residence in 2013 via the Entrepreneur visa scheme. Adam says:

> "Opportunities for entrepreneurs are abundant in New Zealand. This is a country of small businesses. All the elements required for the Entrepreneur visa immigration scheme to succeed are in place, including honest business brokers; strong business banking and law sectors; the ease of registering and establishing a new business with the government; support from the tax authority; and support from the immigration authority. We made our decision to purchase an existing business after looking at dozens of available oppor-

---

[13] https://www.immigration.govt.nz/new-zealand-visas/options/start-a-business-or-invest

[14] http://www.doingbusiness.org/rankings

tunities. They differed in how much capital was required and what skills were needed, but in all cases we were confident that if we fulfilled our immigration application requirements, New Zealand would grant us those highly coveted visas. And they did! We love our adopted country with all our hearts."

New Zealanders in general are an entrepreneurial bunch. Half the cars on the road sport graphics advertising a family business and small local shops pop up constantly. What makes New Zealand such a great environment for small and medium-sized businesses? Starting a business is easy, first of all. Most everything required can be done online, in minutes (see: business.govt.nz). Also according to World Bank data[15], New Zealand is #1 in ease of getting credit, registering property, and protecting minority investors.

Most employers in the United States are burdened to provide health insurance for their employees, costing an average of over US$12,000 annually[16] for a family—a huge expense and rising each year. Not so in New Zealand. Everyone here on a long-term visa is covered by the country's public health system (possibly supplemented with private health insurance paid for individually).

[15] http://www.doingbusiness.org/data/exploreeconomies/new-zealand/

[16] https://www.zanebenefits.com/blog/faq-how-much-does-it-cost-to-provide-health-insurance-to-employees

Which is to say, health insurance is not a typical expense for New Zealand employers. (See Step 22 for more on New Zealand healthcare.)

The New Zealand government offers a number of programmes for helping people get new businesses off the ground (there's a Business Training and Advice grant and the Flexi-wage programme is another). Even if you immigrate to New Zealand on a standard Work to Residence visa, New Zealand is a supportive place to start or run your own business one day.

Step 5:
Sail to New Zealand (or Fly)

Once we made the decision to emigrate to New Zealand the old-fashioned way—by boat—we spent the next few months searching for the perfect ride. Eventually we found it in Portland, Oregon: a sturdy 38-foot sailboat we re-christened *Wondertime*. We moved on board a year later when our daughters were 18 months and 4 years old. A year after that, Michael quit his job, we secured the lock on our small closet-sized storage unit, and we sailed out of Olympia, Washington, USA, for the final time.

We spent our first months in British Columbia, Canada, getting used to travelling on board our new home. We sailed around Vancouver Island where we saw otters and whales and sea lions and bears. We departed Canada in late summer, making our way down to Southern California for autumn. With hurricane season officially over, we crossed the border into Mexico and spent a warm Christmas with other kid boats.[17] The next few

---

[17] If you think you might want to sail with your kids too, check out the book I co-wrote, Voyaging With Kids: A guide to family life afloat (voyagingwithkids.com). All you need to know to take your family to sea, too!

months, we explored the Sea of Cortez and read-
ied our boat to cross the Pacific Ocean.

On 17 March 2012 we shoved off the North
American continent for good, pointing our bow
towards the South Pacific. We sailed and sailed
and sailed, read books, played games, caught fish
and rain. We crossed the equator and drank beer.
Just 26 days later, we arrived in the luscious Mar-
quesas Islands of French Polynesia. For the next
six months we made our way across the South Pacific, our focus on our New Zealand prize.

On Thanksgiving morning (1:30 a.m.), we
dropped our anchor in the Bay of Islands, New
Zealand, just 18 months after casting off from our
dock in Washington and nearly four years after
Michael Palin helped us decide to do it.

Of course, you could catch a plane and fly here
too.

But what about all your stuff? It was easy for us,
as nearly everything we owned was aboard our
sailboat. (We left only a few boxes of photos and
mementoes remaining in storage in the United
States.) Before you go, decide what's important to
bring with you. Many people come to New Zealand with only the bags they carry. Dishes, towels,
and other sundry items are probably not worth the
cost of shipping. Some people ship favourite furniture and other personal items. If this is your case,
get quotes as soon as possible to help decide how
much and what to bring, then start packing. It can
take months for ocean shipments to arrive.

One thing you must bring to New Zealand is money. I am often asked how much someone needs to budget for life in New Zealand. Of course, there are too many variables for me to give a single answer. How big is your family? How frugal are you? How much do you like chocolate and wine and macadamia nuts? (The latter are NZ$70 per kilo here.)

For what it's worth, we've been tracking our family-of-four's expenses recently and our basic budget breaks down as follows (all in NZ$):

- Rent: $425 per week (3 bedroom apartment in Wellington region)
- Electricity: $200 per month
- Internet (unlimited data plan): $95 per month
- Cell phone: $25 per month (each)
- Car insurance: $40 per month
- Petrol: $70 per tank
- Groceries: $1000 per month
- Eating out: $250 per month
- Netflix: $10 per month

Everything else varies (alcohol, medical fees, entertainment, clothing, school fees and activities, kids' toys, books, etc.). So, if you won't have an income right away, make sure you have enough reserves to get by until you do.

Step 6:
Obtain Visitor Visas
Upon Arrival

When we checked our boat into New Zealand the morning after we arrived, a Customs Officer came aboard and stamped each of our passports with a Visitor Visa, valid for three months. They'll do this for you at the airport too. But do check the current visitor visa regulations[18] on the NZ Immigration website as New Zealand requires visitors from some countries to arrange for a visitor visa before they arrive (people from "visa waiver countries" are not required to apply before arrival).

There are other requirements too, such as proving you have enough funds for the length of your visit and holding an onward ticket. (Our boat was the proof we needed that we could leave the country when our visas were up.) Look into all of these before you arrive, just as you would travelling to any foreign country. After the initial three months is expired, visitor visas can typically be extended for another six months, for a total of nine months.

---

[18] https://www.immigration.govt.nz/new-zealand-visas/options/visit

If your job search was successful back in Step 3, you might already have your work visa in hand. Or, if you've applied to study or have a working holiday, you'll already have your visa sorted before you arrive. If this is the case, skip ahead to Step 8: Things to Do When You Arrive and Step 15: Rent a Home.

Step 7:
Get a (Temporary)
Place to Live

*A*lthough it's a lot more work, more expensive, and more exciting than flying, bringing our home—our boat—across the Pacific with us was sure handy when we arrived in New Zealand. All we had to do was sign up for a marina slip in Auckland which took about five minutes. When we secured the dock lines in our new slip, we were home.

Assuming you don't plan to sail here or secure housing before you arrive, the following list includes ideas for temporary accommodation, besides staying with friends or family or (at the other end of the budget scale) pricey hotels, while you find your longer-term place.

Rent or buy a camper van or motorhome

Unless you already have a job nailed down and need to get to work, this is a great time to see your new country. With kilometres of beautiful and rugged roads, motorhome parks, Department of Conservation campgrounds, and countless free places to camp, we highly recommend seeing New Zealand by road. There are heaps of rental options from cosy vans to spacious RVs;

we recommend thl group (thlonline.com) and
Jucy (jucy.co.nz). If you are looking to use a
camper for longer-term, say more than a month,
buying one is probably a more cost-effective option (daily rentals can run NZ$150 per day and
up for motorhomes). You can find all sizes,
types, and price ranges on Trade Me. On my
blog (bit.ly/NZmotorcamping) are more tips for
motor caravanning affordably in New Zealand.

Short-term rentals

You can find a place to stay for a few days or a
few months using the same website you may
have used back home: Airbnb.co.nz. We also
recommend using New Zealand's local version,
Bookabach.co.nz. We've used this website a
number of times to find wonderful places to stay
on holiday. It's also worth checking out the website Couchsurfing.com; you might find a free
place to stay *and* some new friends.

Backpackers or hostels

You can find excellent backpacker accommoda-
tions and hostels all around New Zealand in
both cities and rural areas. They are not only for
the 20s set either; many of them have rooms
suitable for families and can be a very affordable
option over standard hotels. Another boon is
that you'll get to meet a lot of other travellers
too...who are probably in their 20s. In other

words, a lot of fun (see: newzealand.com/int/ backpackers).

House sit

Kiwis love to travel, usually heading overseas for some or all of their four weeks (or more) off work each year. Many of these travelling Kiwis need people to watch over their homes and pets and chickens while they are away. This is a perfect solution for homeless immigrants. Check out kiwihousesitters.co.nz and housesittingnz.co.nz, two websites full of housesitting opportunities.

Step 8:
Things to Do When You Arrive

When we arrived in New Zealand, we'd never lived in a foreign country before. But New Zealand isn't all that different from the United States or the U.K. when it comes to the basics of life. There are grocery stores and warehouse stores and banks and cell phone service providers. Concerning these aspects, moving here felt a lot like moving to another city or state in our birth country. Use the following list to make your move as easy as can be.

Grab a cell SIM

We found signing up for cell phone service far easier than in the United States. New Zealand providers have the same contracts and monthly paid plans, but most providers also offer easy, affordable, no-contract pre-paid cell plans. If you have an unlocked phone you can buy a new SIM card right at the airport when you arrive, put some money on your account, and your phone is ready to go. If you don't have a phone or yours is not compatible with New Zealand's cell system (GSM, UMTS, HSDPA and LTE networks are used here) you can grab a cheap phone to use in the meantime. For NZ$30 per month, a pre-paid plan will get you around 200 minutes

of calls within New Zealand and 1 GB data (and
many plans now roll-over the leftovers at the
end of the month). As long as we take advantage
of WiFi when it's available (such as at libraries
and cafes when we're not home) we find this
more than adequate. You can always top-up
with more minutes and data if necessary.

Get an address

You are going to need an address to receive mail
and packages, have your car registration sent,
sign up for library cards, etc. A P.O. box will do,
but keep in mind that in New Zealand many
packages are sent via courier and they don't de-
liver to P.O. boxes. Living on our boat at the marina, we used the marina address for courier
package deliveries. We also signed up for a P.O.
box at the local PostShop for receiving mailed
letters, magazines, and packages. Now that
we're living in a flat, everything gets delivered
right to our door.

Open a bank account

All you need to open an account at many banks
in New Zealand is your passport. In some cases
you will need proof of address (which can be
tricky until you've secured permanent housing).
ANZ offers to set up an account[19] for you before
you arrive in New Zealand so it's ready to go

---

[19] http://www.anz.co.nz/personal/migrants-travel-foreign-
exchange/microsite/en/open-a-bank-account/

when you get here. You can use your home bank's ATM or debit cards here of course, but you might get charged foreign transaction fees. New Zealand uses the EPTPOS system for instant electronic payments—even the tiniest food truck will accept EPTPOS. It seems cash is rarely used here! Most employers use direct deposit for wages so having your account all set up will make getting paid that much easier when the time comes.

Transfer funds

Once your bank account is ready to go, transfer funds from your home bank using a money transfer service or wire. Talk to your home bank about options. We set up an account with Western Union and it was very easy and quick to fund our New Zealand bank account.

Get a New Zealand driver licence

The New Zealand Transport Agency allows you to drive here on a foreign licence for 12 months after arriving (after which you'll need to apply for a New Zealand driver licence). There are a number of requirements to meet, including that your current licence is valid and it's in English (or you have a translation)[20]. New Zealand, like the U.K., is a left-hand drive country. You've probably also seen photos of the narrow, wind-

---

[20] https://www.nzta.govt.nz/driver-licences/new-residents-and-visitors/driving-on-nz-roads/

ing roads with only randomly-placed barriers
between you and a mile-high cliff. That really is
what roads are like here so drive carefully!

Consider buying a car

If you are basing yourself in central Auckland or
Wellington you may not need or even want a
car. Larger New Zealand cities have good public
transportation (particularly Wellington with its
fantastic train system). New Zealand cities are
compact—it's easy to get around just by walking. But if you want to expand your range, buying a car is a simple process and quite affordable
(this does not include petrol; it's currently going
for about NZ$2 per litre, or $8/gallon). Brand
new cars are available, but most cars on the road
are used Japanese imports. New Zealand imports thousands of used cars from Japan each
year. These imports, most fewer than 10 years
old and with relatively few kilometres on them,
are deemed too "old" for Japan's strict environmental standards.

We've found Hondas and Toyotas often sell
for half of what a similar car would fetch in the
United States. We're currently driving a 10-year-
old Honda Fit with just over 80K kilometres on
the odometer for which we paid approximately
US$4,000. Start your search on Trade Me. In
Auckland, visit a local car fair to view and buy
cars sold by private individuals and mum-and-
pop dealers (the Ellerslie Carfair (carfair.co.nz) is

held every Sunday, for example). It's simple to register your new-to-you car by popping into your local PostShop or VTNZ. Make sure your car has a current Warrant of Fitness (WoF)[21], a safety check performed once a year (many sellers will have this done before the car is sold). While New Zealand does not require car owners to secure third party insurance, it's obviously a good idea to sign up. It's easy to do online and takes only a few minutes.

[21] https://www.nzta.govt.nz/vehicles/warrants-and-certificates/warrant-of-fitness/

Step 9:
Obtain Police Certificates

When applying for any visa valid for 24 months or longer (visitor, study, work, or any residence visa), New Zealand requires proof that you have a good character[22]. All this means is that you'll need to supply a police certificate demonstrating your lack of (serious) criminal history from any country of which you are a citizen and any country in which you've lived (how recent your time in another country was, and the length of time you stayed, to require a certificate from that country depends on the type of visa applied for). Certificates must be less than six months old when you submit your visa application. Don't wait until the last minute to request a certificate, but don't do so too soon either. All the details on the Immigration NZ website, including country-specific guidelines for obtaining police certificates can be found at immigration.govt.nz/new-zealand-visas/apply-for-a-visa/tools-and-information/police-certificates/.

Obtaining a police certificate from the FBI in the USA was the most difficult part of the entire im-

---

[22] You can find their definition of "good character" at:
https://www.immigration.govt.nz/new-zealand-visas/apply-for-a-visa/tools-and-information/character-and-identity

migration process for us to stumble through but I will tell you the secret to getting this done quickly and efficiently. We learned it the hard way.

First, you (and your partner and any children over 17) will probably need fingerprints. You can obtain these while in New Zealand, but the fingerprints may have to be on the form used by the respective country. If you require a police certificate from the United States, print several copies of the FD-258 Fingerprint Form. Again, check the guidelines on the Immigration NZ website for any other countries you need certificates from. Bring the fingerprint forms and your passport to any New Zealand Police station outside of Auckland. They will take two sets of fingerprints from you, certify them, and give them to you to submit to the agency in the respective country (the FBI in our case). Call ahead first to make a fingerprinting appointment. If you are in Auckland, several New Zealand Post retail outlets now handle fingerprinting.

If you need a United States certificate from the FBI, DO NOT request your certificate directly from the FBI! Going this route can literally take months to get the results back as you are competing with all the people buying guns in the United States (and in the meantime your new employer will be waiting impatiently for your work visa to get completed). When Michael accepted his job offer, he popped into the tiny Bay of Islands police station, grabbed his fingerprints, then mailed them off to the appropriate FBI office and waited. And waited. He contacted them to see what the hold-up was and learned it would be at least another six weeks before they'd be able to send the record to him (there truly was a run on gun background checks that month).

We then looked into the second option, using an FBI-approved channeler to get the required check done. It turned out that by paying (a lot) more money we could have Michael's certificate 24 hours after the channeler received it. After obtaining (yet another) set of fingerprints, we sent them along with application overnight via DHL to the company in the United States. Indeed, the very next day the link to the secure document arrived in our email inbox. Done! (A huge shout-out to Accurate Biometrics for getting Michael to work on time.)

Tips for travellers

To apply for a residence visa, a police certificate is generally required from any country (in addition to your country of citizenship) in which you've lived for 12 months or more within the past 10 years. Thankfully, Immigration NZ has recently loosened the guidelines for temporary visas (such as work or student visas valid for 24 months or more); now a certificate (other than that of your citizenship) is required only if you have lived in a country for five or more years since the age of 17.

It's always easiest to obtain this while you are in a country, but if you've already left the country, or if obtaining it in country means your certificate will be dated outside the 6-month window of application submission, follow the guidelines on the Immigration NZ website to obtain one.

In the event you try but are unable to obtain a police certificate from a country, Immigration NZ has a process whereby you can instead make and provide a separate statutory declaration stating this. This will enable you to submit your application on the basis that you will submit the police certificate(s) if and when you obtain them.

Our Canadian friends Rick and Kyra, who also moved to New Zealand via sailboat, found themselves in this very situation, having previously spent 16 months in Mexico on their boat:

> "It was very difficult to get our police certificates from Mexico, even though we tried following the Immigration NZ directions. Some of that was the language barrier (though I get by in Spanish); some of it was getting documents sent in a timely manner (use a courier—not post—if dealing with Mexico as postal service is very slow. We had to resend documents that had expired by the time they were received!) Finding a lawyer in Mexico to act as power of attorney took over 20 tries; only two responded to my inquiries. A friend of a friend was eventually able to connect us with a great lawyer in Mexico

City. We ended up writing a statutory declaration and submitted our work visa applications without the Mexican police certificates in order to make the deadline. We were hoping for the best. (It's better to send an application in on time and send missing information later according to the immigration officer I spoke with on the phone.) The certificates did eventually arrive and we sent them in once we had the documents officially translated. That process, including lawyer fees (we got a bargain at NZ$500) was around NZ$1000. We had not planned ahead for New Zealand and some of our other documents were also difficult to retrieve as a result. Another tip, if you're struggling, it doesn't hurt to contact the embassy of the country you are trying to get documents from; we got great advice from the Mexican embassy!"

Step 10:
Get a Job

If you didn't land a job back in Step 3 or you're not running your own business by now, it's time to grab a job offer. In order to get a work visa in New Zealand, you—or your employer-to-be—has to prove there's no one already in New Zealand that can do the job. Don't let that worry you, however, as it's a lot easier than it sounds. Here are four ways to do it:

Get a job that's on the Long Term Skill Shortage List

The skills and occupations on this list are defined as having "a sustained and on-going shortage of highly skilled workers both globally and throughout New Zealand". In other words, Immigration NZ has already determined there's a shortage of people in New Zealand to do these jobs. If you have the skills and experience to get a job in one of these fields, you would apply for—and hopefully be granted—a Long Term Skill Shortage List work visa[23] that is valid for up to 30 months. This is a Work to Residence visa, meaning that if you hold the LTSSL job for two

---

[23] https://www.immigration.govt.nz/new-zealand-visas/apply-for-a-visa/about-visa/long-term-skill-shortage-list-work-visa

years, you (and your family) can apply for residence visas if you meet all other requirements (age, character, health, etc). All skill shortage lists can be found at skillshortages.immigration.govt.nz.

Get a job that's on the Immediate Skill Shortage or Canterbury Skill Shortage Lists

The occupations on these lists are considered to be in temporary short supply. (The Canterbury list is for occupations in critical shortage in the Canterbury region due to the 2010 and 2011 earthquakes.) If your profession is on one of these two lists, you may be granted the Essential Skills work visa[24]. This is considered a temporary visa (although it can be valid for up to five years). It is not a Work to Residence visa, but you may be able to apply via another residence visa programme (such as the Skilled Migrant Category). Note: If your job is not on any skill shortage list, you may be granted an Essential Skills work visa if your employer can show they've made "genuine but unsuccessful efforts to find a suitable New Zealand citizen or resident for the position".

Get a job with an accredited employer

An accredited employer is one approved by Immigration NZ to offer employment to anyone

---

[24] https://www.immigration.govt.nz/new-zealand-visas/apply-for-a-visa/about-visa/essential-skills-work-visa

who meets their skill requirements, even if those are not on the skill shortage lists. Assuming you meet all other visa requirements, you're likely to be granted a Talent (Accredited Employers) work visa[25], valid for up to 30 months. This is a Work to Residence visa; you and your family may be able to apply for residence after 24 months of working for an accredited employer.

Get a talent

The final work visa option is for those whom Immigration NZ defines as having "exceptional talent in their field of art, culture or sport". You'll need a sponsor to vouch for your talent (this can be an individual, organisation, or government agency, as long as they are of "national repute" in the field). For example, if the All Blacks want to hire you to play rugby for them, you're probably golden. You may then be granted the Talent (Arts, Culture and Sports) work visa[26], which is a Work to Residence visa.

Recruiters & other middle-persons

With New Zealand's relatively small workforce, you might be surprised at how many middlemen there are between you and your dream job. For

[25] https://www.immigration.govt.nz/new-zealand-visas/apply-for-a-visa/about-visa/talent-accredited-employers-work-to-residence-visa

[26] https://www.immigration.govt.nz/employ-migrants/hire-a-candidate/support-a-candidates-visa-application/talent-work-to-residence-visa-arts-culture-sport

most skilled work (ICT, engineering, healthcare) whether you apply from an ad on Seek.co.nz or directly to the company itself, a recruiting firm or inside human resources recruiter will likely screen your resume first.

Michael's recent job search went something like this:

1. Submit CV/resume, cover letter, and application
2. Callback from recruiting company (usually a quick phone screening)
3. In-person meeting with recruiter
4. Informal meeting with company manager (coffee chats at a local café are popular)
5. Formal interview
6. Informal meeting with top manager
7. Offer! (usually presented by the recruitment agency)

Got an offer?

Congratulations! Now is the time to negotiate. Be sure to reference one of the many New Zealand salary surveys available for free from Hudson[27], Robert Walters[28], or Hays[29] prior to discussing salary with anyone—including during your phone screening with the recruiter. They will usually ask what your salary requirements are. Be prepared and don't undervalue yourself. Your employer-to-be will give you a written job offer which should

---

[27] http://nz.hudson.com/salary-hub/salary-guides

[28] https://www.robertwalters.co.nz/salarysurvey.html

[29] https://www.hays.net.nz/salary-guide

include the job description, pay details, and conditions of employment. Sign it to accept when you agree with the stated terms. If the employer is accredited, they'll give you a form with this information as well. For Essential Skills and Long Term Skill Shortage List visas, they'll also need to provide the Employer Supplementary Form (INZ 1113).

Step II:
...But Where?

For such a small country—in terms of both land mass and population—New Zealand has a lot of options when it comes to lifestyle. You can live smack-dab in the middle of a bustling hipster city or right in the bush in the middle of nowhere. You can grab a lifestyle block, complete with chickens and a couple of sheep, within commuting distance to most cities. Like to surf? It's hard to find a town—large or small—that doesn't have a surfing beach nearby. While it's definitely easier to get an ICT job in one of the larger cities, if you're lucky enough to be in healthcare or construction or teaching, for example, choosing where to focus your job search can be even more difficult than finding a job. Maybe you already know what type of place you prefer. Or perhaps you're like us and you love the vibrancy of cities *and* the peace of rural life. Here are some thoughts that may help you narrow down all the choices to find your ideal spot in New Zealand.

Big city life

New Zealand's largest cities are Auckland and Wellington on the North Island, and Christchurch on the South Island. We spent our first years in

Auckland (pop. 1.5 million), living right downtown. That was a matter of chance more than anything; our friends who helped refer Michael to job prospects had lived there and we were able to dock our boat where Michael could walk to his office every day. We still love Auckland: the weather is warm and sunny, it's got a great Polynesian vibe, we met people from all over the world, and the beaches are truly stunning. But it suffers from a lot of the same problems that most large cities face these days (traffic jams and expensive housing to name the top two).

Eventually we chose to relocate to Wellington. This tiny, vibrant city has a quarter of the population of Auckland and far less traffic (the extensive train system helps keep cars off the road) but it's got all the good aspects of a big city: museums, restaurants, parks. Plus it has the best craft beer in New Zealand! Your third big city option is Christchurch (pop. 381K) down on the South Island. This city is still recovering from the destructive earthquakes of five years ago, but it's been steadily rebuilding ever since (providing lots of jobs). You can feel the sense of community coming together there. The natural beauty of the South Island really is as grand as all the photos show and you'll be right next to it all in Christchurch.

Small city life

If a smaller city is appealing, check out Hamilton (pop. 224K), Tauranga (pop. 131K), Napier-

Hastings (130K), and Palmerston North (pop. 83K) on the North Island. On the South Island, Dunedin (pop. 117K) and Nelson (pop. 65K) are the next largest cities after Christchurch. Want to live in the most southern city in New Zealand? Then you'll want to head to Invercargill (pop. 50K). Traffic is rare in any of these places and housing is far more affordable than in the larger population centres. The main attraction of small city life is that you'll be minutes from amazing beaches and native bush walks...and will probably see someone you know there.

Rural life

If you are interested in a rural lifestyle, drive out of any population centre for about 20 minutes. (Keep driving out of Auckland for about an hour.) From there, you can either keep going, or you can set your roots down and commute into the city if that's where your job lies. "Lifestyle blocks" are popular; a ¼ acre section with room for chickens, a goat, a cow, maybe a sheep or two, and plenty of room for a garden. If your job is not tied to a city, there's plenty of acreage to be had; most of New Zealand is wide open space. We currently live in a quiet seaside village 30 minutes north of Wellington city, accessible via motorway and the train system. Just on the other side of the hill from us, a short walk away, are sheep farms and horse ranches. We can pile everyone in the car and be hiking in native bush within minutes. We love

how easy it is to access a variety of settings from
our home.

Island life

New Zealand is more than just the North and
South Islands. In fact, the country is comprised of
33 islands (but only 13 of them are populated). If
you are feeling like the North and South Islands
are just too big, check out one of the smaller islands. Waiheke Island is so close to Auckland that
residents commute to and from the city. Great Bar-
rier Island, in the Hauraki Gulf and accessible by
ferry to Auckland, is chock full of native bush,
wild and beautiful. Kawau Island feels remote and
like you've gone back in time...but it's only an
hour from Auckland by road and foot ferry. If you
really want to get away, check out Stewart Island,
south of the South Island. If true isolation is what
you seek, the Chatham Islands (pop. 600) can be
reached by air, about 500 miles east of Christchurch.

Step 12:
Gather Evidence

Throughout the immigration process, you might be asked to provide evidence of, well, everything from being born to getting a promotion at your last job. Actually, collecting these documents really is Step 0 as it's best to get started gathering everything together long before you depart for New Zealand. But if you make the same mistake as we did and leave all the documents you need behind in your storage unit, don't despair. Just apply for copies to be sent to you in New Zealand. For example, my alma mater mailed a brand new university diploma to me for US$20.00 (I then had a copy certified by a Justice of the Peace). But if you can, bring it all with you, even things you think you might not need.

Here are the documents you should collect:

Evidence of qualifications relevant to your job offer

You'll need to provide evidence of formal training and degree(s) held that are relevant to the job you've been offered. Collect official transcripts, original or certified copies of diplomas, and copies of any certifications or licences you hold. You'll need to check the New Zealand Qualifications Authority (NZQA) to see if each international qualification is recognised and therefore exempt from verification. If it's not, you'll need to have the NZQA assess the qualification for equivalency to New Zealand qualification standards[30].

Evidence of work experience relevant to your job offer

Michael collected letters, on company letterhead, from his past ICT employers confirming his dates of employment, position, and duties. He also included copies of letters of commendation he'd received over the past few years. Finally, he collected copies of past payslips and copies of previous employment contracts. Letters of reference and tax records are other examples of evidence of work experience.

Evidence you have met/can meet registration requirements

If your job requires occupational registration (such as nurse, electrician, and lawyer), Immigration NZ requires "evidence you can meet the relevant registration requirements before we will grant a work visa".[31]

---

[30] http://nzqa.govt.nz/qualifications-standards/international-qualifications

[31] The full list of registration authorities in NZ can be found at: https://www.immigration.govt.nz/new-zealand-visas/apply-for-a-visa/tools-and-information/tools/occupational-registration

Proof of marriage

If you're married or in a civil union (and happily, New Zealand recognises both opposite and same sex couples), you'll need to provide an original or certified copy of your marriage or union certificate for any visas based on partnership status (such as the Partnership-Based work visa or any family residence visa). We did not have this with us in New Zealand and were able to order a certified copy from the county in which our marriage was registered. It took a few weeks to receive via postal mail. But this is only one piece of the partnership puzzle (see Step 18 for more on proving your relationship is a genuine one).

Proof of births or adoptions

Collect one for everyone (adults and kids). These are required to apply for extended visitor or student visas for your children, as well as for family residence visas. This proof will also serve to document you're 55 or younger, a requirement for residence visas.

Step 13:
Get Examined

The final bit of evidence you'll need to provide is of your good health[32]. You don't need perfect health, but you can't be a danger to the health of other people in New Zealand (in other words carrying tuberculosis). Applicants may also be denied due to having health conditions that will cost New Zealand's health system too much money. When you submit your first visa application, the report must be less than three months old, so you'll want to time this accordingly.

There are often two parts to the medical exam for adults: a chest X-ray to show you don't have tuberculosis (TB) and a full medical examination including urine and blood tests. A chest X-ray is only required if you are from or have spent more than three months in a country that does *not* have a low incidence of TB (or in other words, a country that is *not* on the list of countries with a low incidence of TB[33]). If you are from the United States, hold off until you are able to get all exams and tests done in New Zealand; you will save heaps of

---

[32] https://www.immigration.govt.nz/new-zealand-visas/apply-for-a-visa/tools-and-information/medical-info

[33] https://www.immigration.govt.nz/new-zealand-visas/apply-for-a-visa/tools-and-information/medical-info/countries-with-a-low-incidence-of-tb

money over what medical centres in the United States will charge. There are many New Zealand clinics that will do the required tests and exams all at once, what is typically called an "immigration medical" package. The usual fee is NZ$250 for adults, NZ$75-150 for kids. It's a great value for a thorough medical exam!

Finding a clinic is simple. Google "new zealand immigration medical" and you'll be greeted with a host of options, especially in Auckland. Two that we rate highly are Symonds Street Medical Centre (ssmc.co.nz) and Victoria Park Medical Suites (vicparkmed.co.nz)—both are also great GP practices. You can search all providers—both in New Zealand and overseas—approved by Immigration NZ to complete medical and chest X-ray certificates at: immigration.govt.nz/paneldoctors.

The four of us spent a morning at one such clinic in Auckland and got all our tests and exams done in one go. Since our daughters were both under 10 years old, they only required one exam each. Michael and I got the full package: health history and physical exams, blood and urine tests, chest X-rays (having spent the past 18 months in countries *not* on the list of low incidence tuberculosis countries). A couple of days later we were notified via email that our completed medical certificates were submitted to Immigration NZ via the NZimed electronic system. We were ready for the next step.

Even if Immigration NZ determines you or someone in your family does not have an "ac-

ceptable standard of health" they might grant a
medical waiver if all other visa conditions are met.
There are only a handful of situations where a
medical waiver cannot be granted (such as requir-
ing kidney dialysis or full-time care). In a situation
where heath may be an issue, it's well worth con-
tacting a licensed immigration adviser to discuss
the options.

Step 14:
Submit Work Visa Application

*W*ith your signed job offer and Employer Supplementary Form INZ 1113; education and experience evidence; and police and health certificates in hand; it's time to apply for your new work visa.

Back in 2013, Michael trekked up Queen Street in Auckland with his pile of documents—including his completed Work Visa Application (INZ 1015)—to the Immigration NZ office. There, he stuffed everything and his passport into an envelope and popped it into the appropriate submission slot at the office. He could have mailed it all, but he wanted to be sure it was received promptly; his employer-to-be was waiting eagerly for him to start work.

But that was then and times have changed. Now it's possible to apply online for most types of work visas. You'll need your documents scanned to PDF format. (Each document should be its own separate file. For example, a 3-page document should be a 3-page PDF file). All documents must be translated into English and certified by an independent translator. You'll include both original and translated versions with your application(s).

You'll also need a photograph of your face (JPG format) that complies with Immigration NZ's acceptable photo format (full-front view of the face, head and shoulders, looking straight at the camera, neutral expression, eyes open, mouth closed and head straight). There are a number of smartphone apps that will format a passport-style image for use online and/or printing. You'll also need to provide your residential address so your passport and documents can be returned to you via secure post. Some Immigration NZ offices will allow applicants to pick up their documents.

The final step of the online application process is to pay your application and migrant fees. Payment can be made using a Visa- or MasterCard-branded credit card. Easy peasy.

Once your online application is submitted and the fee paid, you'll receive instructions for sending your passport, along with a form to print and include. Currently, if sending from within New Zealand, your passport will go to Auckland's Northern Area Documentation Office. If sending from outside New Zealand, be sure to specify exactly where you are applying from, to ensure you are directed to send your passport to the correct office.

Because Immigration NZ realises employers are waiting for work visas to be issued, applications are usually processed within a few weeks. You can keep tabs on your application status via the online account you set up when you submitted your application. If Immigration NZ needs any further documents or clarification from you, they'll contact you directly via email or phone. During our experience, we found all the immigration officers exceedingly polite and helpful. I got the impression they really want to issue visas! If they request additional information or clarification, get it to them quickly to keep the ball rolling. Michael hadn't signed his job offer when he submitted the copy with his application. When he received an email from the immigration officer handling his application asking for him to sign it (proof he'd actually accepted the offer), he signed the original form, scanned it, and emailed it back to the officer the same day.

Once your work visa is approved, you'll get a shiny label affixed inside your passport as proof of your eligibility to work (and you'll also need it to access things like health services). But while you are waiting, if you haven't already found a place to live, now's the time.

Step 15:
Rent a Home

I do hate to be the bearer of bad news, but you've reached the most difficult step on your move to New Zealand: finding a place to live. As I mentioned earlier, in New Zealand's largest cities and towns, housing costs, as a percentage of average wages, are high. There is usually competition for any flat (apartment) or house that goes on the market to rent or buy. And when you do find a place, dealing with property managers can be a real drag as their main priority is keeping the property owner's investment in good nick. Finding an abode can take some time, but don't despair, you'll eventually find a place to call home. Read on for information that may help.

Renting in New Zealand

Most people rent a flat or house when they move to New Zealand, at least while they get settled in. Purchasing a home is an option, but the process is quite involved and so I've limited the scope of this book to renting. Should you decide to rent, you're in good company: over 50% of the populations in cities rent homes (35% average throughout the country)—and both numbers are growing rapidly. If you are interested in buying a home, you'll be interested to know that anyone can purchase property in New Zealand; you don't even have to be a citizen or resident.

But upon first arriving, renting gives you the flexibility to get to know your new city and decide where you might want to put down longer-term roots. Despite being high, in most areas rental rates are still half of what a mortgage on the same property would be, and that comparison doesn't even take into account the added ownership costs of rates (property taxes) and homeowner's insurance. You might be able to tuck your savings away to buy a home in the future (or save for more travel, as we like to do). If you didn't bring your furniture with you, or don't feel like shelling out for everything all at once to fill empty rooms, know that furnished rentals are available.

Finding a home

Just like buying a car or finding a job, Trade Me is the place to begin your search for a home. You can narrow your search by region, district, and suburb; number of bedrooms and bathrooms; price and type (apartment, house, etc.). If you didn't haul your whole family with you to New Zealand and simply need a room to call your own, check out Trade Me's flatmate listings of people seeking to share their houses or flats.

A typical rental listing will state when the property is available to move in, the preferred number of tenants, what's included in terms of furnishings and whiteware (appliances such as fridge and washing machine), parking availability, and whether pets are allowed. Rents in New Zealand are listed on a per week basis; we pay our rent fortnightly—two weeks' worth at a time (not monthly, as in the United States). Also, unlike the United States and Europe, there are few corporate-owned rentals available. Most rentals, even flats in the city, are owned by private individuals who contract with a property manager to handle the lease, maintenance, and all other tenancy details. There are some owners who choose to manage their rental properties themselves.

Your first contact will likely be with such a property manager. There are excellent property management companies (that are attentive to the needs of both property owners and tenants) and there are terrible ones. The Trade Me listing for an available rental will show who the property management company is and I recommend you check out their Google reviews. There are certainly a few that you'll want to avoid entirely. Obviously, take reviews with a grain of salt; it's common knowledge that people who are disgruntled with a company tend to let everyone know and satisfaction doesn't usually give people cause to share their experience. But you can discern important information from the types of complaints (unresponsiveness to maintenance issues and incorrectly lodging and refunding bonds would be red flags).

If proximity to a good school is a housing consideration, you'll want to research the schools in the area you're planning to live. Most schools have enrolment zones, meaning a student can only attend if they live on one of the streets identified in a school's zone. You can search for schools and their enrolment zones (if applicable) at this website: nzschools.tki.org.nz. This one is a good place to research schools in general: educationcounts.govt.nz/find-school. (For more information on schools, skip ahead to Step 21.)

Once you find a home you're interested in, the property manager or owner will either give you a private showing or invite you to an open showing on the weekend. Once you decide on a home you want to rent, you'll fill out a rental application. Employment details, rental history, financial status, and references may be required. The management company may also run a credit check (this will be limited to credit extended and debts owed in New Zealand). There is usually no application fee. Most properties receive multiple applications, so this is the time to cross your fingers and hope the property manager/owner selects you for the tenancy. In the meantime, keep your eyes open for other possibilities.

Life as a tenant

New Zealand houses and apartments are notoriously cold and damp, especially as you make your way further south, in the direction of Antarctica. Double-pane windows are rare and I don't think insulation was available until the mid-1980s. Most dwellings still have little to no insulation, but times are changing. New laws mandate that landlords must provide a statement to a renter detailing the location, type, and condition of insulation in a rental home. (By July 2019, they'll actually be required to install it.) Be sure you review this statement. Providing heating is optional, but landlords are required to provide an electrical outlet in the main living area for a tenant to plug in a space heater (and rack up high winter power bills). Central heating is rare, but finding a rental with an efficient heat pump is possible (and a bonus). With the rental market increasing, more landlords are installing heat pumps to make their properties more attractive to renters. Unfortunately, before signing a rental agreement, you'd be wise to check for signs of water leaks and serious mould issues, additional traits of New Zealand housing.

The Residential Tenancies Act prohibits discrimination against tenants in accordance with the Human Rights Act. This means landlords cannot refuse to rent to someone because of their gender, marital status, religious or political beliefs, age, family status, and more. Despite this, the property manager/owner will select the tenant they like best. If you feel you've been discriminated against, contact the Tenancy Tribunal (tenancy.govt.nz/disputes) which handles disputes between tenants and landlords, or the Human Rights Commission (hrc.co.nz).

Once you're selected as a tenant, congratulations! You'll next head to the property manager's office to sign lots of forms and to pay fees. In New Zealand, the typical lease period is one year. Sometimes a shorter lease (three or six months) will be offered, especially in the case of furnished rentals set up for shorter-term tenants. All tenants normally pay a refundable bond (two, three, or four weeks' rent) and often a non-refundable "letting fee" (equivalent to one week's rent) is payable for the property manager's services.

Before you sign the actual lease, read through the Tenancy Services website (tenancy.govt.nz), particularly the section on tenancy agreements. There are laws on what landlords may and may not include in a tenancy agreement, but property managers will still try to sneak in clauses that are simply not legal. Read your agreement carefully to make sure that's not the case. There is often room for negotiation as well. Our current flat was listed "no pets allowed" but we asked if they'd make an exception for our cat and they did.

Once you're in, expect an inspection by the property manager every three months. As Americans, we find this very intrusive. But we're getting used to it; we understand that our owner wants to be sure their property is being well-kept. And we see that this inspection is a face-to-face opportunity for us to bring up any maintenance issues that need to be addressed. With luck, they'll be fixed promptly by the owner.

If a disagreement arises between you and the property manager or owner and you're unable to resolve them directly (for example, they still haven't fixed your broken hot water heater after three weeks and aren't returning your calls), follow the guidelines on the Tenancy Services disputes process website (tenancy.govt.nz/disputes). The Tenancy Tribunal will help mediate and enforce a solution if necessary. The Tenancy Tribunal may also come into play at the end of the lease period, such as in the event you and the property management company cannot come to agreement about what constitutes normal wear and tear, or whether your cleaning efforts are sufficient to merit a return of deposit. It's an excellent service for both tenants and landlords.

Unlike in the United States, many rentals in New Zealand do not include refrigerators, dishwashers, and washing machines (few people in New Zealand own a clothes dryer—there's plenty of sun for that). Tenants must bring their own along with their furniture. You can find used whiteware on—you guessed it!—Trade Me. There are lots of buy/sell/trade local Facebook groups popping up (also an excellent source for used furniture).

Welcome home!

Step 16:
Learn the Lingo

*W*hile you're waiting for immigration to issue your new work visa, this is a good chance to bone up on some Kiwi-isms. The mix of Polynesian and Pākehā (European) immigrants has resulted in a slang totally unique to these islands at the bottom of the world. You'll soon hear these terms used by your work mates and you won't want to let on that you have no idea what they're talking about.

Aotearoa: Original Māori name for New Zealand and still in wide usage. It means "land of the long white cloud".

Kiwi: A nickname for a New Zealander. It's also the name of a New Zealand native nocturnal flightless bird and a fruit (the Chinese gooseberry).

Kia ora: Hello in te reo Māori (Māori language). Here's a list of 100 other Māori words that are handy to know: nzhistory.net.nz/culture/maori-language-week/100-maori-words.

Cheers: Thank you or good-bye.

Ta: Thanks. As in, You: "Here's my train fare." Conductor: "Ta!"

Arvo: Afternoon. "Come on over this arvo for tea."

Choice: Awesome.

Sweet as: Cool or neat. "That concert was sweet as." (Although any adjective can be used: "That ice-cream is cold as" or, "It's dark as tonight" or, "That new taco truck is cheap as.")

Good as gold: Yes or affirmative.

Good on 'ya: Well done.

She'll be right: It will all turn out just fine.

Heaps: A lot.

Bach: Small rustic holiday home, usually at the beach. Short for (and pronounced like the first part of) "bachelor".

Silly season: When the entire country is on holiday, from Christmas Eve to the end of January.

Holiday: Vacation. Also used to refer to actual holidays (like Christmas, Waitangi, and ANZAC days).

Sausage sizzle: BBQ'ed sausages, served on margarine-smeared white bread.

Bring a plate: Bring a dish of food (such as for a potluck).

Jandals: Flip flops or thongs. Worn year-round in Auckland, nine months of the year everywhere else.

Sunnies: Sunglasses.

Crook: Sick. "I'm leaving work early...feeling crook."

Flash: New or fancy. "Have you seen his new car? It's totally flash."

B.Y.O.: Specially licenced restaurant where patrons can bring their own alcohol.

College: High school.

Uni: University.

Whanau: Family (in te reo Māori).

Mates: Friends.

Bloke: A guy. Probably one who loves Rugby.

Bro: Friend. Maybe even someone's brother.

Bogan: What we'd call a red-neck in the United States A derogatory term for a lower-class, unsophisticated person. Usually proud of it.

Dole: Unemployment benefit. (You'll be eligible for the dole as a resident.)

Fortnight: Two weeks.

Hire: To rent. "I need to hire a car for the week."

Judder bar: Speed bump.

Ute: Small truck or 4-wheel-drive.

Petrol (station): Gasoline (station)

Boot: Car trunk.

Gumboots: Boots.

Jersey or Jumper: Sweater.

Togs: Swimming suit.

Tramp: To hike.

Stuffed: Tired.

The bush: Wild, native forest land. "We went for a long as tramp in the bush and now I'm stuffed."

Long drop: Outdoor toilet, built over a hole in the ground.

Scrogin: Trail mix of nuts and dried fruit.

Plaster: Band-aid.

Rubber: Pencil eraser.

Op shop: Thrift or second hand shop (short for "opportunity shop" often fundraising for Red Cross or local hospital).

Tip: Rubbish or recycle depot.

Aluminium: Aluminum.

Morning tea: Mid-morning break.

Afternoon tea: Mid-afternoon break.

Tea: Dinner. "I'm going to be late for tea—can you keep it warm for me?"

Feed: Meal. "I'm starving—can't wait to tuck into a good feed."

Jug: Kettle for boiling water, nearly always electric.

Hob: Stovetop burners, gas or electric.

Dairy: Small corner convenience store. "We're out of toilet paper. I'm heading down to the dairy to get some."

Takeaway: Food or coffee to go. "I'll have my flat white takeaway. Ta!"

Chips: French fries. (Never, ever call them French fries or you'll get laughed at).

Chippies: Potato chips.

Fizzy drink: Soda.

Lollies: Any sweets or candy.

Biscuits: Cookies.

Ice block: Popsicle.

Courgette: Zucchini.

Capsicum: Green, red, yellow, or orange pepper.

Coriander: Cilantro.

Chook: Chicken.

Mince: Ground meat (usually beef).

Kumara: Sweet potato.

Marmite: Favourite spread made from yeast extract. You're supposed to spread it on toast but we think it smells like dog food. (Vegemite is Oz's version—just as bad!)

Oz: Australia.

0 (Zero): Pronounced "oh", same as the letter "O".

Zed: How Kiwis pronounce the letter "Z".

Step 17:
Go to Work

Keep your eye out for the red and yellow courier truck. When it arrives with your shiny work visa affixed inside your passport, it's finally time to go to work!

First, apply for an IRD (Inland Revenue Department) number (see: ird.govt.nz/how-to/irdnumbers). You'll need this number to give to your employer so they can submit your income taxes at the correct rate to Inland Revenue. If you haven't done so already, get a bank account ready for your income; most employers will directly deposit your pay into it. By the way, your income tax owed will automatically be deducted from your pay and submitted to the government. You won't be required to file an income tax return at the end of the year unless you are owed a refund (for charitable donations, for example); you received other, unreported income; or you face another taxable event. For all the details on taxes in New Zealand see ird.govt.nz.

One of the best things about New Zealand is that all employees—whether part-time, full-time, fixed term or casual—are entitled to four weeks of paid annual leave. Leave time will accrue as you work and by the end of a year you'll be entitled to take a month off! Nearly everyone in the country takes their holiday at one of two times: in the middle of the year (to escape the New Zealand winter for the Northern Hemisphere summer) or during the Silly Season, which starts around Christmas Eve and ends at the end of January (also when the kids are on summer school break). Your employer may give you the option to split your weeks up.

In addition to your four weeks of paid holiday, you are by law also entitled to 11 public holidays per year. And if a holiday falls on a Saturday or Sunday? No worries—thanks to Mondayisation policy you'll get your day off on the following Monday (or Tuesday as the case may be).

The public holidays in New Zealand are[34]:

- New Year's Day (1 January)
- Day after New Year's Day (2 January)
- Waitangi Day (6 February: Celebrates the 1840 signing of the Treaty of Waitangi, New Zealand's founding document.)
- Good Friday (day before Easter weekend, date varies)
- Easter Monday (day after Easter weekend, date varies)
- Anzac Day (25 April: Commemorates Australian and New Zealand Army Corps

---

[34] Take note of the down under date format! Day goes before month, then year. You aren't likely to be confused by 25/2/2016, but 1/10/2016 has the potential to cause real problems. Just remember it's January 10 if you're reading a U.S. date and 1 October if you're reading a Kiwi date. Does that clear it up? No? Sorry.

[ANZAC] members killed in war and returning servicemen and women.)

- Queen's Birthday (1st Monday in June,
  though her actual birthday is 21 April. Don't
  ask me why she has two.)
- Labour Day (4th Monday in October)
- Christmas Day (25 December)
- Boxing Day (26 December)

Finally, each region of the country has an anniversary day that is also observed (usually with a
day off of work for many). For example, Auckland's anniversary date is 29 January and Nelson's
is 1 February.

If that's not enough time off and you get sick of
working, remember that you're also entitled to five
paid sick days per year.

But wait…there's more! If you add a child to
your household (either by birth, adoption, or fos-
ter [applied to children under 6]) the primary
caregiver may be eligible for 18 weeks of paid pa-
rental leave (as long as you've been employed or
self-employed for at least 10 hours a week in at
least 26 of the 52 weeks leading up to your due
date or date the child comes into your care). The
primary caregiver may even transfer some of their
leave to their partner so she/he can spend time
with the new child. (On 1 April 2016, the amount
of leave was increased from 16 to 18 weeks. Aren't
you glad you live in New Zealand now?)

That so much time off work is available to New
Zealanders is an indication of the value this cul-

ture places on a healthy work/life balance. Sure, just like anywhere else there are Kiwi workaholics who check email at all hours of the day, but working more than 40 hours a week is unusual and rarely an expectation. If a New Zealander is not headed to the pub for happy hour at 17:00, you'll find them at the beach with their families walking, kayaking, sailing, or kite boarding. Kiwis take their weekends seriously too: unless the weather is particularly bad, most will be found outside, doing something active in nature.

Step 18:
Prove Your Relationship

Michael's receipt of his work visa not only allowed him to finally start earning a paycheck, it opened the door for me to apply for the Partner of a Worker work visa[35]. Unlike the Essential Skills and Work to Residence visas, the Partner of a Worker work visa is not tied to a specific job. Though I've spent the past 10 years working part-time as a self-employed writer, with this visa in hand, I could have taken a position with any employer, part- or full-time. Even while not working, the visa allowed me to remain in New Zealand as long as Michael's work visa was valid.

To apply for a Partner of a Worker work visa, you must include with your application the Police Certificate(s) (Step 9) and Health Certificates (Step 13) you already obtained. You'll also need one more thing: proof that you and the original work visa holder are in a *genuine and stable relationship*.

Unfortunately, a marriage certificate isn't proof enough for Immigration NZ. You must provide evidence that you and your partner didn't get hitched just for the purpose of acquiring New Zea-

---

[35] https://www.immigration.govt.nz/new-zealand-visas/apply-for-a-visa/about-visa/special-work-visa-for-partners-of-work-visa-holders

land visas. Immigration NZ defines a genuine and stable relationship as follows:

> "We need to be satisfied that you and your partner entered your relationship with the intention of it being maintained on a long-term and exclusive basis. We also need to be satisfied that your relationship is stable and likely to last."

Immigration NZ wants proof that you live together and for how long (and if you've lived apart, the reasons for doing so). They want evidence that you share finances, knowledge of children you may have and parent together, and that other people vouch for your relationship.[36]

Some or all of the following may be used as evidence of your partnership:

- marriage or civil union certificates
- birth certificates for any children you share
- cards, letters, emails, and social media conversations
- photos together
- evidence that others recognise your relationship
- evidence you make decisions and plans together
- evidence you parent together
- evidence you spend leisure time together

---

[36] For full details on partnership requirements visit:
https://www.immigration.govt.nz/new-zealand-visas/apply-for-a-visa/tools-and-information/support-family/partnership

- a joint rental agreement or home loan
- mail addressed to you together at the same place and time
- joint bank accounts
- evidence you own assets together
- joint credit cards or hire purchase agreements
- joint utilities accounts, such as power or phone bills

Besides our marriage certificate, we collected records of joint home-ownership, boat documentation and moorage agreements, bank statements, our daughters' birth certificates, cards from friends addressed to both of us, a letter from a close friend attesting to our relationship, and even a magazine article about our family from a few years back. Collect anything you can think of that shows you live and love together and intend to keep doing so.

Step 19:
Apply for Partner of a
Worker Work Visa

To apply for the Partner of a Worker work visa, the partner holding the original work visa
will need to complete the "Form for Partners Sup-
porting Partnership-Based Temporary Entry Application" (INZ 1146). The applicant needs to
complete the "Partnership-Based Temporary Visa
Application" (INZ 1198). All application materials
must be submitted by mail or in person to the appropriate immigration office. These include your
fees (credit card information on your application
form or check), passport-sized colour photo-
graphs, Medical and Chest X-ray certificates (or
eMedical Reference Code), Police Certificate(s),
and passport.

But what if Immigration NZ concludes your relationship is a sham? This is what happened to our
friends Rick and Kyra. Kyra told me the story:

> "Even though Rick and I had been togeth-
> er for 20 years, and were married for 16 at
> the time of our application, we were
> asked to supply more information as
> proof that we were still in a relationship.
> We had included a lot of information, but

were a little light on the most recent year
(despite giving a link to our blog that
documented our travels up to and while
living in New Zealand). It can be challenging to come up with stuff like utility
bills (we make our own electricity and
water, seeing as we live aboard a boat)
and we don't have a tenancy agreement
(another thing they asked for), again because we live aboard. We had to get creative: the marina wrote a letter confirming
we had been renting a mooring, members
of the community who'd gotten to know
us offered to write letters confirming our
relationship, and so on. In the end, Immigration NZ finally believed we were
genuine partners!"

Step 20:
Get Kids' Visas

By this time, your kids' initial, three-month visitor visas may be close to running out. If you or your partner don't have a work visa by now, then it's time to extend everyone's visitor visas (in most cases up to a total of nine months). But, I'll assume all the steps have gone flawlessly and you or your partner is off to work by now. In that case, it's time to apply for longer-term visas for your kids. These will likely be valid for the same length of time as your work visas.

A dependent child of a work visa holder is considered a domestic student and can attend preschool, primary, and secondary school fee-free (since their parents are now tax-paying New Zealand workers). Immigration NZ states:

> "School-aged dependent children need a student visa to be able to attend primary, intermediate or secondary schools, and do not pay international fees unless they are in tertiary study. Children younger than school age can apply for a visitor visa. A student visa is not needed to attend preschool in New Zealand."

Most kids in New Zealand begin primary school when they turn 5 (even on the day of their birthday!). School attendance is not compulsory until kids are 6, but most parents are eager to start them full-time (and most kids are eager to start too...school is pretty fun in New Zealand). But to do so, you'll first have to submit the Student Visa[37] application for any child aged 5 or older. This one can be done online or via paper application (INZ 1012).

You'll need your child's medical certificate (and chest X-ray, if required, for children over 10) and passport-style photograph, and police certificates if aged 17 or older. If the primary working parent holds an Essential Skills work visa, you'll also need to provide evidence that you meet the minimum income threshold to be able to support your family. (As of August 2016, this amount is NZ$36,850.44 per annum gross.) Evidence can be in the form of a copy of the employment agreement and the income of both parents can be combined to meet the threshold.

Once Immigration NZ issues your child's student visa, your child will be able to enrol in school as a domestic student (you'll do this next in Step 21). Until then, they may be able to attend as an international student and pay the accordant fees.

---

[37] https://www.immigration.govt.nz/new-zealand-visas/apply-for-a-visa/about-visa/dependent-child-student-visa

Our oldest daughter was 7 when she received her student visa; we enrolled her to start Year 3 at our local primary school. Our younger daughter was only 4, not yet eligible for a student visa. For her, we applied for the Child of a Worker Visitor Visa[38]. This extended her visitor visa to match the term of Michael's initial work visa (30 months). We enrolled her in the local kindy (preschool).

Our family applied and was approved for residence before our youngest turned 5. But, if we'd not done so, or had our residence application been denied, we would have applied for her student visa right before she turned 5 so she could join her sister at primary school.

---

[38] https://www.immigration.govt.nz/new-zealand-visas/apply-for-a-visa/about-visa/dependent-children-of-work-visa-holders-visitor-visa

Step 21:
Send 'Em to School

*W*e've found—through our experience at the two different primary schools our kids have attended—New Zealand schools to be innovative, staffed with dedicated and hard-working teachers, and buzzing with happy, active kids. Though schools do follow the New Zealand Curriculum (NZC), standardized testing is minimal and unobtrusive. Primary kids receive nearly 90 minutes of recess each day, plus formal outdoor physical education most days. Our excellent school experience is one of the main reasons we love living here. The following tips will help you send your kids off to school in New Zealand.

Kindergarten ("kindy")

3- and 4-year-old kids typically attend kindy (preschool). The New Zealand government pays for the first 20 hours a week of early childhood education (called "20 hours ECE"). Unless the kindy runs all day, it is essentially free. The 20 hours ECE can also be used for other approved programmes, such as play centres, childcare centres, and some home-based care. Kindys, just like all schools, may request a small parent donation (more on this below). Our youngest daughter attended a kindy in Auckland for a year. The play-based, friendly programme was a delightful experience for all of us. It's also a great way to meet other families; we are still friends with several we met at kindy.

Primary school

As I described in Step 20, when kids turn 5 they typically begin primary school. (School is compulsory between the ages of 6 and 16.) If a 5-year-old student starts school in the middle of the school year, they'll join a new-entrant class or Year 0. They'll join a Year 1 class at the start of the new school year. Some students attend "full primary" from Year 1 through 8 before going on to secondary school. Others attend a "contributing primary" from Year 1 through 6. These students will attend an intermediate school for Years 7 and 8 before going on to secondary school.

Secondary school

Years 9 to 13 are considered secondary school ("college"). How long a student attends secondary school depends on the NCEA (National Certificate of Educational Achievement)[39] level they wish to achieve. There are three levels available, with level 3 being the highest and the one required by most universities. We like this system as it recognises that all kids do not have the same aptitudes, goals,

[39] http://www.nzqa.govt.nz/qualifications-standards/qualifications/ncea/

and ambitions and allows them to get the most out of school to address their personal futures, whether they're heading into the trades or working towards a PhD. There are also a number of secondary schools in New Zealand that have International Baccalaureate (IB) programmes, a challenging qualification recognised by universities around the world (see: ibschoolsnz.org.nz).

Enrolment zones

Most primary and secondary schools in major cities and high-density areas require students to live within a specified zone to enrol. These schools usually require proof of address, such as a tenancy agreement or power bill. Again, here's the website to view enrolment zones for schools in your area: nzschools.tki.org.nz. If a school has spaces left after all local students are enrolled, they may hold a lottery (typically once per year) for out-of-zone students who wish to attend.

School terms

Nearly every non-tertiary school in the country follows the same term schedule. There are four terms, each 10-11 weeks long with a two week break in between. Term 1 usually begins the first week in February and Term 4 wraps up in the week before Christmas. The summer holidays are six weeks long before the next school year starts in February.

Public vs. private

Like most anywhere, New Zealand has public (government-funded) and private/independent (tuition-based) schools. Private schools are not required to follow NZC standards, although many choose to do so. There are also former private schools that are now state-integrated. These schools have chosen to integrate into the state system but retain their "special character". An example of a state-integrated school would be the Rudolph Steiner (Waldorf) schools located around New Zealand. Since the property and buildings are still privately owned, the school will charge dues which can be nominal to significant (one Steiner school we toured requested nearly NZ$4,000 per year per child). Many private and state-integrated schools are identified with a religion, such as Catholic or other Christian denomination.

Researching schools

Every early childhood, primary, and secondary school is reviewed periodically by the Education Review Office (ERO). When researching schools, read through both the most recent and past ERO reports; these reports detail the strengths of a school and the challenges it's facing, as well as goals for improvement. The length of time between reports is also telling. If a school is reviewed every 5 years, that indicates the ERO office is confident the school is achieving well; a school that's reviewed every year or two may be under close scrutiny for a reason. Reports can be found via the ERO website (ero.govt.nz) or through educationcounts.govt.nz/find-school, which lists extensive data for each school, including how well students are meeting the NZC standards.

Donations, fees, and uniforms

Schools in New Zealand ask families to contribute a donation to supplement what the school receives from the government. Parent donations help to pay for everything from additional teachers (allowing for smaller class sizes) to sports programmes to more art supplies. While the donation is voluntary, pressure is high to contribute at least some amount. You will also probably be asked to pay fees for field trips, camps, and special events. If you're interested in more fundraising, each school has a P.T.A. and they'd love for you to join. Each student must provide their own stationary pack (notebooks, pencils, etc.). Some schools— particularly secondary—are moving to the bring-your-own-device (BYOD) model, meaning that an iPad or Chromebook may be on the stationary list as well. Nearly all secondary, intermediate, and private schools require students to purchase and wear the school's official uniform. Many primary schools do not have a uniform.

Homeschooling

New Zealand allows families to homeschool, but only if the parent can prove their child will be "taught at least as regularly and as well as in a registered school". If you pass the application process, the Ministry of Education will grant you a Certificate of Exemption (of the compulsory schooling requirement) and you can begin homeschooling[40]. A separate application is required for each child. Once approved, you'll be eligible for the annual home education supervision allowance to help offset the cost of books and materials (currently NZ$743 for the first child, NZ$632 for the second and so on). It's estimated that under 2% of children in New Zealand are homeschooled, but that number is growing. There are a variety of New Zealand homeschooling groups on Facebook. Local groups exist as well; members share everything from support in homeschooling to coordinating classes for students. Auckland Home Educators is a one such group.

---

[40] http://parents.education.govt.nz/secondary-school/secondary-schooling-in-nz/home-education

Step 22:
Get Healthcare

*A*t some point, especially if you have kids, a member of your family is going to require medical care in New Zealand. Here's what you need to know.

The New Zealand health system

As I mentioned earlier, everyone in New Zealand—from tourists visiting for a week to New Zealand citizens—has comprehensive injury coverage through the ACC. If your health problem is due to an accident (no matter how small—it could be something as minor as a sliver in your thumb) the costs of treatment are usually 100% covered. We love this system. If you do need to see a health provider due to an accident, be sure you make it clear that you'd like the charge to go through the ACC system. Some providers charge additional fees but they are always significantly less for ACC claims.

If your work visa is valid for two years or more (or you're a New Zealand resident or citizen), you and your dependents are eligible for publicly funded health and disability services in New Zealand, including prescription and medical device access (full details on New Zealand's health system, including eligibility details are here: health.govt.nz/new-zealand-health-system).

If you are not eligible for publicly funded health services (if your work visa is only valid for a year, for example), be sure to take out a travel insurance policy that will cover you in New Zealand. While the costs of health care are considerably less than in places such as the United States and Canada, you could still easily run up a bill of thousands of dollars if, for example, you require surgery. IMG Global is one such company offering international health insurance for people living and travelling overseas.

Those eligible for publicly funded health care in New Zealand can also choose to purchase private health insurance to supplement. Such a policy will give you access to more choices of (private) doctors, specialists, and medical centres. In some cases, you'll be able to access treatment sooner than the longer waiting lists of publicly funded providers. A comprehensive policy will often cover other medical fees such as GP (general practitioner) visits and prescription charges. For what it's worth, we've not purchased private insurance. I've found access to publicly funded specialists to be more than adequate. The consultation fees GPs charge for visits (NZ$35-$50) and prescriptions (NZ$5 per script for a 3-month supply) are nominal. Kids under 13 are fee-free for GP visits and prescriptions.

A private health insurance policy may also include routine dental and vision care—two items not currently covered for adults over 18 in the publicly funded system. (Kids 17 and under are eligible for free dental care and vision checks.) With few exceptions, if you are over 18, you're responsible for all dental care costs—from exams to root canals. If you need a lot of dental treatment, it's usually cheaper to fly to Fiji or Thailand…and get a vacation at the same time.

Accessing medical care

Your GP will be your first contact for accessing non-emergency medical care. In order to receive subsidised (reduced) consultation fees, you'll want to enrol at a local GP clinic. Google is a good place to find one, or you can search for all registered doctors at mcnz.org.nz/support-for-doctors/list-of-registered-doctors/. When you enrol, you'll be asked for proof of eligibility (your passport with valid visa) and medical history. Until you are enrolled, you can visit any GP or medical centre (depending on availability) but the fees will likely be higher as the visit won't be subsidised. You'll be assigned a NHI (National Health Index) number to identify you and your records in the national system; make a note of this identifying number.

Your GP can write you prescriptions to fill at any chemist (pharmacy). PHARMAC (Pharmaceutical Management Agency; pharmac.govt.nz) is the agency that maintains the list of what medicines and medical devices are publicly funded. (If you require something that's not funded, it is possible to apply for Special Authority. Otherwise you'll need to pay the higher cost or choose a funded alternative.) Your GP will also refer you to any specialists as needed (a diabetes centre, for example). Once the specialist clinic receives the referral, you'll eventually get a notice in the mail with your appointment time. To see what specialist services and hospitals are available in your area, make a note of your local District Health Board or DHB. This is the organization responsible for providing and funding certain health services for people in their district.

If you seek medical care anyplace other than your GP office (such as at a hospital emergency clinic or urgent care clinic) bring your passport along to prove your publicly funded status. However, if you forget, the billing office will remind you and you can often send a copy later. I once took my youngest daughter to a children's emergency department at night with a wheezy, croupy cough. Of course, I forgot to bring our passports. The woman who checked us in gave me an envelope to post a copy of my daughter's passport later. To us, as Americans, the New Zealand health billing system is shockingly simple: we pay whatever fee is due right when the service is performed. We've never received a single bill in the mail.

Step 23:
Live Kiwi Life

*W*ith Michael off to work, the kids at school, and myself seated in my writing chair, we soon settled into Kiwi life. This essentially means we took—and continue to take—weekends very seriously. While we spend some of them simply puttering about at home, our favourite weekends are the ones we spend exploring. New Zealand's relatively small landmass means you can cover a lot of ground in just two or three days. Following are some ideas for exploring your new country and generally enjoying Kiwi life.

Book-a-bach

As you may have done in Step 7 for your temporary accommodation, book a small (or large) vacation home for the weekend. The country is full of interesting places to stay, from 100-year-old historic cottages to modern city apartments. (See: bookabach.co.nz or airbnb.co.nz.)

Hold a sausage sizzle

What you need: a BBQ, a bag of Heller's sausages, a loaf of white bread, margarine, grilled onions, Wattie's tomato sauce, and a bunch of new friends. Optional: a sunny day, beer, and an old couch on your back deck. Smear leftover bread with margarine or Nutella and sprinkle with hundreds-and-thousands (rainbow dot sprinkles) to make "fairy bread".

Try an adventure
Bungee jumping, white water rafting, black water rafting, caving, zip lining, luging, skiing, sailing, scuba diving, surfing, and sky diving are not just for tourists. Give it a go. (We're still working up to all of these except for sailing.)

Pick up a sport
Weekend sports are not just for kids: there are adult rugby and cricket leagues, roller derby, sailing and cruising clubs, karate, and lots more. While some people are more competitive, the spirit of simply having fun prevails. Or, if you'd just rather watch, go to a rugby game—you're not considered a true Kiwi until you do.

Go swimming
You'll find Kiwis swimming in the ocean almost year-round. If you're still working up to that, head to one of the local swimming pools. New Zealand takes its pools seriously—they are amazing facilities. Many feature Olympic-sized lap pools, hot pools, saunas, and kids' pools complete with water slides, waves, and waterfalls. They are truly world-class.

Go to a park

New Zealand takes great pride in its parks—both large and small. Towns and cities have huge amounts of green space and some of the kids' playgrounds are the best we've seen in the world. Kids of all ages enjoy walking, picnicking, socializing, and simply lounging around parks and botanic gardens around the country.

Take a hike

New Zealand is crisscrossed with hiking tracks, in city and bush. Take a stroll through a city botanic garden or head out a little further for a walk in the woods. There are walks suitable for every ability imaginable (even shorter, wheelchair-accessible walks). Whether you want to walk for 20 minutes or all weekend long, there's a track for you.

Clean up, catch vermin, or plant a tree

Join a local environmental group and clean up a beach, help plant native trees, or set traps to catch invasive rodents that take down native birds. There are heaps of local groups determined to keep New Zealand green...and a good thing too.

Get a library card

Pop into your local library with proof of residence or employment and grab a shiny new library card. Get access to print books and magazines, CDs, DVDs, eBooks, Zinio magazines, puzzles, and much more. Our family visits our local library every Thursday afternoon to stuff a bag full of books for the week. Also check out the social events available, such as knitting circles, author talks, and preschool story times. We love the community libraries in New Zealand.

Learn te reo Māori

The language of New Zealand's first immigrant group, the Māori, is still widely in use. It is considered the Maori people's greatest *taonga* (treasure) as their language embodies their history, values, and hopes for the future. You can study on your own (nzhistory.net.nz/culture/maori-language-week) or enrol in a local class; these are often held free for the community. Learn more about Māori culture by visiting a *marae* (a Māori community meeting house) and if you're lucky, a *hangi* (feast cooked with heated rocks in a pit oven). While you're there, practice your *hongi*, the Māori greeting of pressing one's nose and forehead to another's. Known as "the breath of life" the greeting represents the god Tāne breathing life into the first human woman, Hineahuone.

Go to a festival

If it's the weekend, there's probably a festival on. Whatever you're keen on: food, coffee, beer, wine, whisky, arts, literature, poetry, dance, fashion, film, music, comic con, comedy, busking, LGBT pride, fringe, love, the sun, walking, sports, cycling, cars, boats, planes, pets, flowers, kites, lights, Scottish games, Polynesia, history and…well, there's a festival for you[41].

Eat

Mince and cheese pies, sausage rolls, feijoas, whitebait fritters, Bluff oysters, green-lipped mussels, roast lamb, fish & chips, pavlova, Pineapple Lumps, hokey pokey ice cream….

Visit a farmer's market

The best place to buy fresh, local, in-season produce is not at New World, Pak'nSave, or Countdown (New Zealand's chain grocery stores), but at your local farmer's market. Nearly every town large and small has one (although some are seasonal). The Wellington farmer's market is legendary, covering Te Papa Museum's entire parking lot in summer. In December, we buy buckets of strawberries at Paihia's market in the Bay of Islands…out of this world! If you need fruit and veges on other days of the week, pop into a roadside stand. Their offerings are usually fresh, local, and sold at a fraction of the grocery store prices.

---

[41] For a comprehensive list of festivals in NZ see:
http://www.thecuriouskiwi.co.nz/festivals.html

Visit a museum

While you are at Wellington's farmer's market, drop into Te Papa, New Zealand's national museum. Come back the next day too; it's so large and there is so much interesting information and things to see, you really need a couple of days to take it in. Auckland's War Memorial Museum is outstanding. (Don't let the name fool you: there's tons more to see other than war-related exhibits. Check out the greenhouses at the domain, too.) Only have a few hours? There are hundreds of smaller museums all around New Zealand. From quirky to shocking, they're full of fascinating New Zealand history and artefacts.

Go see animals

New Zealand's got some pretty interesting wildlife, but some of it's also really good at hiding. The best places to see critters are at one of the great zoos, aquariums, wildlife parks, nature centres, or farm parks. But you really can't beat driving through sheep country (it's really all sheep country) during lambing season. And glowworms—we never get tired of spotting those.

Visit a South Pacific island

You might want more than a weekend to do this, but if the New Zealand winter is getting you down, all you need to do is board a plane and a couple of hours later you'll find yourself in tropical paradise. Rarotonga, Niue, Tonga, Fiji, Samoa, New Caledonia, and Vanuatu are all just a short flight away and each is full of sunshine, white sand beaches, warm ocean, fresh coconuts, and friendly cultures.

Step 24:
Consider Residence

With every member of our family holding a New Zealand visa, each valid for the next 30 months, we started thinking about the next level: becoming residents. Our visas allowed both adults to work, the kids to go to school, and all of us access to funded healthcare. What would New Zealand resident visas grant us?

- **Live, work, study in New Zealand indefinitely.** Unlike our work and student visas, a resident visa does not expire. We'd be able to live and work in New Zealand forever.
- **Work for any company.** A work visa based on a job offer is good only for the position and company stated on the work visa (it is actually printed right on there). A resident visa is not tied to a specific job, allowing holders to work for any employer in the country. With a resident visa, there is no change to status if the visa holder quits a job, is fired, or made redundant. If any of those things were to have happened to our primary work visa holder, he would have had to apply for another work visa when he found another job.
- **Tertiary education.** As residents, my husband and I would be considered domestic

students, allowing us to attend university
and pay only the discounted government
subsidised tuition. While New Zealand trade
school and university tuition has risen in recent years, Kiwis pay a fraction of what students in the United States pay. For example,
2016 undergraduate fees at the University of
Auckland average NZ$6000 (US$4000) per
year of study[42]. This would be a bargain in
the USA for a single quarter! Three years after becoming residents, we'd also be eligible
to apply for student allowances and loans.

- **Public welfare support.** New Zealand has a
strong social benefits system, including
many programmes to help get and keep
people on their feet after losing a job, after
having a baby, when dealing with illness or
disability, or as they age. We'd be eligible for
Jobseeker Support payments should one of
us lose a job or not be able to work due to injury. Working for Families is a weekly payment and tax credit to help lower-income
families. The Accommodation Supplement
helps people to afford housing. Community
Services Cards are available to lower-income
people to offset costs of health services.
Thankfully, we've not needed any of these
services to date, but it's a huge comfort
knowing they are available to us as resident
visa holders.[43]

---

[42] https://uoa.custhelp.com/app/answers/detail/a_id/6858/

[43] For the full benefit list see:
http://www.workandincome.govt.nz/products/a-z-benefits/

- **Retirement.** At age 65, resident visa holders and citizens are eligible to receive New Zealand Superannuation, the (modest) government pension. In the meantime, as residents we are permitted to contribute to our own KiwiSaver retirement investment accounts, supplemented with employer contributions.
- **Voting.** After living in New Zealand for a year as residents, we'll be eligible—no, *required*—to enrol to vote in Parliamentary (national) and local elections. We'll truly have a say in helping keep New Zealand a great country in which to live.

For us, the decision to progress down the resident visa path was easy—we were eager to become full-blown New Zealand residents! The only drawback was the prospect of paying even *more* immigration fees. And, we had another decision to make: Which path to residence would we take?

Option 1: Residence from Work. Michael's Long Term Skill Shortage work visa was a Work to Residence visa, meaning we could simply wait out the required two years while he worked at his ICT job. After that, we could submit our family's resident visa application subject only to the age, health, and character requirements.

Option 2: Skilled Migrant. We could apply to be residents under the Skilled Migrant Category straight away, but only if our combined work experience and qualifications were sufficient (in addition to meeting age, health, and character requirements). To determine whether our combined work experience and qualifications were enough to allow us to take this path to residence, we first had to add up our points....

Note: These were the two resident visa options available to our family. Other residence categories include: Entrepreneur, Investor 1 or 2, Pacific Access Category, Samoan Quota, Relocating Employee, Refugee, Family Stream and more. The Self-Assessment Guide for Residence in New Zealand describes all categories (NZ 1003).[44]

---

[44] All resident visa forms and guides can be found at https://www.immigration.govt.nz/new-zealand-visas/apply-for-a-visa/tools-and-information/forms-and-guides/live-permanently

Step 25:
Add Up Your Points

So, having decided we wanted resident visas, our choices were to wait two years to apply, or to move forward right away. We opted for the latter. That meant applying as a Skilled Migrant[45].

I'll note that it would have been possible to apply for resident visas via the Skilled Migrant Category from the start, when Michael got his first job offer. Why didn't we? Because at the time, Immigration NZ estimated processing times at six to nine months for Skilled Migrant Category resident visa applications. Financially, there was no way that we'd have been able to wait that long for Michael to start working—nor would his employer have been willing to endure that wait!

Before picking up this book, you may have heard about the "New Zealand immigration points system". In short, it's the means by which Immigration NZ determines who is eligible—in terms of skills, experience, and qualifications—to apply for residence under the Skilled Migrant Category. (Note: if you obtain a Work to Residence visa as Michael did, and then decide to wait the two years before applying via the Residence From Work

---

[45] https://www.immigration.govt.nz/new-zealand-visas/apply-for-a-visa/about-visa/skilled-migrant-category-resident-visa

Category, no points are involved.) At the other end of the spectrum, a candidate with enough points can apply for residence under the Skilled Migrant Category *without even a job offer*.

Let's take a closer look at the factors Immigration NZ considers when assigning points.

- **Age.** You and your partner must be 55 or under, but the younger you are, the more points you are awarded (ages 20-29 are prime).
- **Skilled employment.** Do you have a job offer or job in a skilled employment field in New Zealand? Your current job or job offer must be on the List of Skilled Occupations[46]. You are awarded more points if you've held the job for 12 months or more, if your position is on the Long Term Skills Shortage list (LTSSL), and you work outside of Auckland. Even more points are awarded if your work is in a future growth area (in 2016 these are: biotechnology, information communications technology, and creative industries).
- **Work experience.** You are awarded points for work experience relevant to your current skilled employment, based on length of time. More points are awarded if the experience is in New Zealand and if the experience is a LTSSL skill.
- **Qualifications.** Points are awarded for degrees, certificates, and diplomas you hold.

---

[46] https://www.immigration.govt.nz/opsmanual/35165.htm

You get more points if you studied for your qualification full-time in New Zealand and if your qualification is in an area of absolute skills shortage (i.e. on the LTSSL).

- **Do you have close family living in New Zealand?** You'll earn points if you can prove you are related to a New Zealand resident or citizen.
- **Partner points.** More points are awarded to an applicant if their partner is also English-fluent. Points are also awarded based on a partner's current job or job offer in New Zealand, as well as a partner's qualifications.

Add up your points here:

www.immigration.govt.nz/new-zealand-visas/apply-for-a-visa/tools-and-information/tools/points-indicator-smc-28aug

Step 26:
Submit EOI

The first step in applying for residence under the Skilled Migrant Category is to submit an Expression of Interest (EOI). However, to be eligible to submit the EOI, your point tally must be at least 100.

The EOI form can be completed and submitted online with the associated fees paid by credit card. (It's slower, but you can also submit your EOI via paper.) Completing the EOI, you will need to provide detailed information regarding work experience and qualifications, much like a CV. You do not include any evidence of your points claims at EOI submission (this will come later, when you submit your resident visa application). In other words, you'll list your degree, but not submit a copy of your diploma at this point. Details for all family members are required, including children.

Submitted EOIs are entered into a pool and every two weeks Immigration NZ selects which EOIs will be offered the chance to apply for residence. As of late 2016, only EOIs from applicants with 160 points or more are selected. (Previously, EOIs from applicants with 140 points or more were automatically selected; those with 100-135 points were considered individually and of these, EOIs with points for current skilled employment or a job of-fer for skilled employment in New Zealand were more likely to be selected.)

If your EOI is selected you, your partner, and your children will be invited to apply for resident visas.

Step 27:
Submit Residence Application

I'll never forget the day the huge packet of resident visa application forms arrived from Immigration NZ. Our EOI had been chosen from the pool. Along with the pre-populated application forms, a cover letter listed all the evidence we'd need to return with our application—essentially everything we'd claimed points for in our EOI, as well as evidence of our health, character, and English language ability. Since we were dealing with an entirely new immigration department (Residence), we would have to include just about everything we'd sent in for our previous visas. Because we saved all the evidence we'd gathered in Step 12 and Step 18, we simply needed to put it all together. Everything we submitted was original documents; they were later returned with our passports.

It was a really big stack of papers. To organise all of it and ensure we had everything in order, I purchased an expandable slot file folder and sorted everything as follows:

- **Checklist, Application, Fee, Additional Details Forms.** Immigration NZ provided a handy checklist of documents we needed to provide. I included this, along with the pre-populated residence application (completed with the information we'd included on our online EOI), the form with our credit card details to pay the application fee, and Additional Details Forms (INZ 1134) for each family member. Again, we needed recent passport-sized photos for everyone.

- **Birth Certificates.** Original, certified copies for each family member.
- **Passports.** All four of 'em.
- **Medical Certificates.** While our medical certificates were in the NZimed electronic system, we included hard copies of each. These were the same ones we'd already submitted as it had been less than 24 months since submitting our last visa applications.
- **Police Certificates.** Again, these were the same as previously submitted as it had been less than 24 months since our last applications.
- **Employment Agreement.** Hard copy of Michael's signed, current employment agreement.
- **Work Experience.** Detailed information of Michael's skilled work experience, including detailed CV, letters from previous employers confirming dates and positions held, as well as letters of commendation. Also included were copies of payslips and past contracts.
- **Evidence of Partnership.** All the evidence we provided in Step 18 proving our partnership was stable and genuine.

- **Qualifications.** Original or certified copies of high school and college course transcripts along with original/certified diplomas. You might also need to include any New Zealand Qualifications Authority (NZQA) reports, as applicable.
- **Evidence of Future Growth Area.** Michael claimed points for this category as he works in information communications technology. As evidence, he included a letter from his current employer, on company letterhead, outlining his current ICT position, including start date and nature of work.

Again, this list is based on the evidence we needed to support the points we claimed. You or another applicant may be asked to provide different or additional evidence, such as a full or provisional occupational registration and proof of your relationship to family living in New Zealand. Perhaps you'll need evidence that you, your partner, and any children over 16 speak English. (Form INZ 1060 fully explains the many ways to show you and your family meet this requirement.)

Once we had all our evidence collected in our file, we headed back to Queen Street in Auckland and slipped the entire bundle into the "Residence" slot at the immigration office. Residence application...check!

Step 28:
Wait...Wait...and Celebrate

Once you've submitted your residence application, the only thing to do next is...wait. It can take several months for Immigration NZ to process your residence application. (Revisit Step 23 for some ideas for passing the time.)

When Immigration NZ received our application, they sent us an email confirming this. The email included our application and client numbers for future reference. Immigration NZ recorded our evidence and a few weeks later they returned our passports and original documents via mail.

We waited some more.

Due to a health condition (type 1 diabetes), I was notified that my health file was being reviewed by a medical assessor. The immigration officer assigned to our file requested I have some updated blood tests and a dilated eye exam. I got these done within the week and then forwarded the updated results to our immigration officer.

We waited some more.

About a month later, we got an email: our resident visas had been approved! The letter included final instructions to return our passports to Immigration NZ so they could insert our new resident visa labels. We'd also need to pay the Migrant

Levy (in 2013 it was NZ$1000; this funds various settlement support programmes for new migrants). We returned to the immigration office on Queen Street in Auckland, dropped off our passports, and paid the fee.

This time, we waited less than a week. Our passports arrived once again with beautiful new Resident Visa labels inside. Our family could now live in New Zealand forever!

Step 29:
How to Be an Immigrant

Truth be told, we've moved to New Zealand twice: the first time via sea, aboard our sailboat *Wondertime,* the second time via plane, after having returned to live in the United States for a year.

We lived on our boat in Auckland for 18 months when the challenges of living in New Zealand began to overwhelm us. We missed our relatives back home. We got tired of everything being so expensive and some things hard to attain. City life was gnawing at us, but Michael's ICT career kept us from moving to a more rural town. Looking back, it's clear that we were simply homesick. Instead of recognising what's known as "culture shock", we threw in the towel and returned "home".

That turned out to be a huge mistake. We were so glad to be back at first; reconnecting with family and friends truly was wonderful. But back in our old Washington state hometown, we felt like foreigners more than ever. We'd been away too long, traveled too much. And our hearts ached for New Zealand. We were torn in two. After a year back in the United States we made the decision to return to New Zealand. I can happily report that after another 18 months in New Zealand, this country really does feel like our family's home.

The fact is, it's not easy immigrating to *any* country, no matter how welcoming and beautiful and friendly it is. Make sure it's really for you. And if you decide it is, realise that everyone gets homesick. You'll miss what's familiar, including the small things. And the big things: family, friends, language, food, and customs, well, they're even more difficult to be away from.

Even as native-English speakers, looking pretty much like all the other New Zealand-Europeans here, our American accents quickly give us away and the questions begin. Feeling like an outsider can be tiring. Even now, we sometimes long to simply "fit in" again.

It takes months—no, it takes years—to get used to living in a new country. I think Michael and I will always feel like foreigners, no matter how many years pass for us in New Zealand. But our two daughters already think of themselves as New Zealanders, and New Zealand as home. It really is for them, and their futures, that we've gone to all the trouble of moving here after all.

Culture shock

Recognise that there are steps every immigrant goes through to adjust to living in a new country. Everyone feels excited at first, during the honeymoon stage. Everything is amazing and wonderful and you couldn't feel happier about your decision to immigrate.

Then reality hits. Culture shock sets in: differences between old and new cultures come to light. Frustrations with the new culture grow. Homesickness sets in. The gilt begins to wear off. But don't do what we did and throw in the towel at this stage (especially because doing so is very expensive). These feelings will pass.

Integration occurs when you learn to hold both the new and the old culture close. The new language and culture grows familiar. You might jettison some old ways and take on new.

Finally, acceptance. Your old home culture and the new culture of New Zealand combine to become your new way of life. And it all starts to feel right.

Finding a tribe

You don't have to navigate this process on your own. Simply making friends with other immigrants—they don't have to be from your same country—is very refreshing. Talking about your immigration experiences may help you realise that you aren't alone in your process of adjusting. And if you can laugh together about all the silly Kiwi ways, even better.

Many Citizen Advice Bureaus around the country also offer settlement support services for new immigrants, including workshops, seminars, general information, and advice.[47]

There are also regional newcomers groups around the country (see: newcomers.co.nz). These groups hold all kinds of events, from coffee chats to workshops, for people new to New Zealand or just a particular region.

To connect with newcomers online, check out the *New to New Zealand* Facebook page (facebook.com/NewtoNewZealand). There you'll also find many helpful tips for getting used to your new country.

Finally, an excellent book on navigating the integration process is *Culture Shock! New Zealand* by Peter Oettli.

---

[47] CAB's local immigrant support services can be found at:
http://www.cab.org.nz/gethelp/New%20to%20NZ/

Step 30:
Making it Permanent

When you receive your resident visa label, you'll notice that the expiry date is probably "indefinite" (meaning, the visa never expires). But there's a line right above it: "Expiry date travel" and it's likely two years from the visa's start date. This means that during the window between receiving your resident visa and this date, you are free to come and go from New Zealand. But after this date, if you are outside of New Zealand the visa is considered invalid. New Zealand won't necessarily let you back in unless you apply for and are granted extended travel conditions or a second or subsequent resident visa[48].

It's much easier to apply for your Permanent Resident visa after your first two years of residence are up. This is the top-of-the-line New Zealand visa: it never expires and you can leave and re-enter New Zealand as often as you like. Best of all, it's the last one you'll ever have to apply for!

You can apply for permanent residence when you've held your resident visa for two years and

---

[48] https://www.immigration.govt.nz/new-zealand-visas/already-have-a-visa/my-situation-has-changed/live/if-i-am-traveling-and-won2019t-return-before-travel-conditions-on-my-resident-visa-expire-what-can-i-do

can show your commitment to living in New Zealand. This can be done in one of the following five ways:

- You've spent enough time in New Zealand (184 days or more in New Zealand as a resident in each of the 2 years before you apply for permanent residence).
- You have New Zealand tax residence status.
- You have invested in New Zealand.
- You have a business in New Zealand.
- You've established a base in New Zealand through purchasing a home or working full-time.

More information about applying for permanent residence can be found in the printed guide INZ 1176 and at: immigration.govt.nz/new-zealand-visas/already-have-a-visa/resident-to-permanent-resident.

Once you've fulfilled all permanent resident visa requirements, the process of applying is one you'll by now be familiar with: fill out the application form and send it to Immigration NZ along with your passport(s) and fee. Your passports bearing Permanent Resident Visa labels should be returned shortly thereafter...now you can *really* stay in New Zealand forever.

Note: When your passport expires, you'll need to have the visa transferred to the new one. This can be done in person at main immigration branches. Just bring in your passport and...you guessed it: the fee.

Step 31:
The Rest of It...Citizenship

This is it: the final step. After five years of residence, you might qualify to apply for New Zealand citizenship by grant[49]. You'll have to have spent enough time in New Zealand in each of those five years (240 days each year), have maintained your good character, and be able to speak English.

New Zealand allows dual citizenship; our family will be able to hold both our United States passports and New Zealand passports when the time comes. But some countries don't allow their citizens to do so. It's imperative to research the laws in your home country whilst considering a new citizenship. It's not an easy decision and certainly one to consider carefully.

What does citizenship grant that permanent residence doesn't? You'll be able to obtain and travel on a New Zealand passport, for one. You'll also be able to stand for elected offices and have full access to education and economic rights. You could also live and work in Australia thanks to the

---

[49] http://www.dia.govt.nz/Services-Citizenship-General-Requirements-for-a-Grant-of-New-Zealand-Citizenship

Trans-Tasman Travel Arrangement[50] which allows citizens of each country to freely live and work in the other. And don't forget the Cook Islands and Niue—countries in free association with New Zealand, meaning New Zealand citizens can live and work there, and vice versa.

In a few more years, each member of our family will eagerly stand at our citizenship ceremony and swear that, "I will be faithful and bear true allegiance to Her Majesty Queen Elizabeth the Second, Queen of New Zealand, Her heirs and successors according to law; and that I will faithfully observe the laws of New Zealand and fulfil my duties as a New Zealand citizen."

We'll not just have moved to New Zealand...we'll be New Zealanders.

It is an amazing feeling to be a resident of this sweet little country. I've listed many of the tangible benefits, such as beautiful scenery, crazy-affordable college, good jobs, fantastic wine, music, chocolate, coffee.... But what makes us so thankful we can live here as long as we want—even become citizens if we wish—are the intangible benefits. The outrageous kindness and friendliness of nearly every person we meet, the vibrant Polynesian culture, the strong sense of community we're finding everywhere, our kids being given

---

[50] https://en.wikipedia.org/wiki/Trans-Tasman_Travel_Arrangement

the freedom to be kids, a responsive government, the deeply-rooted values that *everyone* deserves healthcare, equality, a living wage, and a chance. We love New Zealand and hope you move here too.

Forms and Guides

Here's a distillation of links to the forms and guides mentioned in this book. (Current as of September 2016)

All types of New Zealand visa forms and guides can be found here:

https://www.immigration.govt.nz/new-zealand-visas/apply-for-a-visa/tools-and-information/forms-and-guides

Visitor Visas

General information:
https://www.immigration.govt.nz/new-zealand-visas/options/visit

Visitor visa forms and guides:
https://www.immigration.govt.nz/new-zealand-visas/apply-for-a-visa/tools-and-information/forms-and-guides/visit

Student Visas

General information:
https://www.immigration.govt.nz/new-zealand-visas/options/study

Student visa forms and guides:
https://www.immigration.govt.nz/new-zealand-visas/apply-for-a-visa/tools-and-information/forms-and-guides/study

Work Visas

General information:
https://www.immigration.govt.nz/new-zealand-visas/options/work

Work visa types:
https://www.newzealandnow.govt.nz/move-to-nz/new-zealand-visa/work-visa/temporary-work-visa

Work visa forms and guides:
https://www.immigration.govt.nz/new-zealand-visas/apply-for-a-visa/tools-and-information/forms-and-guides/work

Investor and Business (Entrepreneur) Visas

General information:
https://www.immigration.govt.nz/new-zealand-visas/apply-for-a-visa/tools-and-information/business-and-investment

Investor and Business visa options:
https://www.newzealandnow.govt.nz/investing-in-nz/visa-investment-options

Investor and Business forms and guides:
https://www.immigration.govt.nz/new-zealand-visas/apply-for-a-visa/tools-and-information/forms-and-guides/invest

Residence Visas

General information:
https://www.immigration.govt.nz/new-zealand-visas/options/live-permanently

Residence visa forms and guides:
https://www.immigration.govt.nz/new-zealand-visas/apply-for-a-visa/tools-and-information/forms-and-guides/live-permanently

Skilled Migrant Category residence visa:
https://www.newzealandnow.govt.nz/move-to-nz/new-zealand-visa/work-visa/skilled-migrant-visas

https://www.immigration.govt.nz/new-zealand-visas/apply-for-a-visa/about-visa/skilled-migrant-category-resident-visa

Residence from Work Category residence visa:
https://www.newzealandnow.govt.nz/move-to-nz/new-zealand-visa/work-visa/residence-work-visas

Other Forms and Guides

Tools and information for meeting criteria:
https://www.immigration.govt.nz/new-zealand-visas/apply-for-a-visa/tools-and-information

Health and Medical forms and guides:
https://www.immigration.govt.nz/new-zealand-visas/apply-for-a-visa/tools-and-information/forms-and-guides/health-and-medical

Nationality specific checklists:
https://www.immigration.govt.nz/new-zealand-visas/apply-for-a-visa/tools-and-information/checklists

Other forms and guides:
https://www.immigration.govt.nz/new-zealand-visas/apply-for-a-visa/tools-and-information/forms-and-guides/other

About the Author

Sara Dawn Johnson, along with her husband and two daughters, moved to New Zealand in 2012 by sailing their home, a 38-foot sailboat called *Wondertime*, across the Pacific Ocean. Sara documented her family's travels at www.svwondertime.com. The Johnson family currently resides in Wellington, New Zealand.

Sara is also the co-author of *Voyaging With Kids: A guide to family life afloat* (2015; L&L Pardey Publications).

For more, visit www.saradawnjohnson.com.

Notes

Made in the USA
Las Vegas, NV
25 November 2020

11454083R00081